THE SOFTWARE ENGINEERING CAREER

ERICK DUARTE

THE SOFTWARE ENGINEERING CAREER

THE WORKFORCE FROM A MILLENNIAL'S PERSPECTIVE

Erick Duarte

CONTENTS

CONTENTS

ABOUT THE AUTHOR

A little bit about myself before digging into the meat and bones of this book. My name is Erick Duarte, I am a current working professional in the software engineering industry. Oh, and I am also a Latino American, from the generation labeled by the media as millennial, just throwing in that info in case that is at all relevant. I come from a middle-class working family and was raised in the city of El Paso Texas, where I also attained a bachelor's degree in computer science from the University of Texas at El Paso, otherwise known as UTEP for short. I began working in the industry in 2016, and have since experienced what it is like working in software engineering as a professional with over six years of experience as of the time of publication of this book, 2022.

From internships to post-graduation I have worked in areas related to or directly dealing with software such as information systems, mobile App development, software chatbot enhancement, backend java development, web, and front-end development, and development operations. These services were performed for companies that may or may not be obvious areas of work for a software engineer, at first hand. I say this because of the nature of the services in which these companies are involved in. In short, the companies I have worked with offer services such as the distribution of ceramic tile, military insurance, telecom websites, college level education and customer services. I think most people can agree that most of the listed services here are not an area a software engineer might first think of working in.

In my quest for opportunity and career growth in tech, I ended up leaving my hometown and have hoped around a few different cities. Nonetheless, I am usually home during the holidays, but long story short I came to the conclusion that in order to evolve in this career one must be where the action is. Now of course there are always alternatives to moving from one's hometown, especially now that remote work is becoming more and more acceptable, but this all depends on the individual's goals.

Well enough about me, this was just a short introduction about who I am relative to the field of software, and we can now move onto the contents of this book. Regardless, a good piece of advice I will give before reading this book, is to take everything I say with a grain of salt. At the end of the day, the decision as to whether or not to transition into a software engineering career soley depends on the individual and their specific parameters as well as goals set by them.

INTRODUCTION

About to graduate high school and looking into software engineering as a potential career? Aspiring to be the next Mark Zuckerberg? Jeff Bezos? Bill Gates? Or perhaps you are what is considered a "middle" aged person, looking to make their third career change? Even if none of the scenarios described apply to you, and you just want to get an idea of what it feels like to be in the software workforce, then this book may be for you. In this book I will utilize experiences as a working professional in the software industry, to describe subjects such as pros and cons of working in the industry. I will also cover things to keep in mind when becoming an engineer and how to break into the industry, as well as branches of software one can expand into. How the

2019 pandemic changed and is changing the way software is built, and the benefits that came with the chaos.

Reasons to transition into a software career vary by person, and at a glance I can offer my two or three cents as to why I chose this career path. In my search for a passion, or more accurately described in my search for a career that I thought would enjoy doing for most of my life, I encountered software development. A choice that I do not regret to the day and I personally would take over gigs I had during college to make ends meet. If you are a tech enthusiast in any form and enjoy day to day technologies that help with tasks like navigating from point a to point b. Getting food delivered to your door or turning on your tv or your vehicle remotely with the simple use of your phone then that in itself may be a good reason enough to consider software engineering as a career. Maybe you are not all that into tech but relative to other choices you've explored this seems like the most interesting or the most bearable. Well the only thing I can say there is that relative to other fields I've worked in, be it as a patient access registrar, forklift operator or a sales associate, software engineering has been heaven on earth for me. That's not to say the jobs I had before weren't good jobs, any job is a blessing in my opinion, but my career in software has been the most exciting, flexible and rewarding not just in terms of compensation but also for personal and professional development. Note that it only beats sales in compensation in my case because I am terrible at selling, it has never been my thing but that is a field with tremendous potential.

Now let's address the big elephant in the room, I understand that there may be people looking to make the transition to a software career simply because of what the pay can do for them. And that is a completely valid reason to pursue a career in something in my opinion, and yes a career in software can offer great compensation and benefits especially for those trying to hold a family together. My career, for example, helped me triple the salary I made prior to my first corporate job as an engineer. Things did not start out that way though and it took a little while to get there, which I will also cover in this book. But to the point, money is an important parameter to take into account in the world we live in, and if that is someone's decision to make a move into software, I respect that and will try to be of as much help as possible here.

If you're an entrepreneur looking to start a software related enterprise, and for that reason you wish to start off as an actual software engineer in the workforce, I think that is a genius idea. Though I currently don't have much experience when it comes to entrepreneurship, I do have close friends that have taken this route and can offer some perspective on what that route looks like. A quick observation I've made from this area, is that it is usually a group or team of software engineers that team up to start their enterprise and tend to work as a whole to move their company forward.

Before jumping into the actual contents of this book, I want to make a note about some words I will use here frequently and interchangeably. For example when I simply say engineering I am talking only about the software engineering field itself unless explicitly stated otherwise. Second, many software related terms will be used here so you may see terms like "web development, programming language, database, machine learning, development operations (devOps), etc" the list goes on and on. With that in mind note that not all of the software terminology will be elaborated upon or defined as they can already be found to be defined in many other books, and or in any search engine. Even so there is no reason to panic, as these terms are purposely used in a manner where its meaning is at least somewhat clear by the end of the sentence. So I recommend reading the full sentence first of where the foreign terminology is found and if it is still not clear, then proceed to look up that word or words relative to the software industry. For example take the word "Full Stack Developer", one can simply paste these three words in google to understand what such a developer does or is. There will be a section describing what paths of software engineering one can take, which will aid in understanding some of the software related terminology used in this book, but no glossary will be provided in this literature, so just bear that in mind. Lastly not all terms will need to be looked up or expanded upon as I feel some of the terms used like "programming language" for example, are self describing and hence the reason they are used as is.

ADVANTAGES OF WORKING IN THE SOFTWARE INDUSTRY

To start off in helping you make the decision, I will first dig into what perks a career in software engineering can offer. The focus will be based on personal experiences or peers experiences, but take note that this is not an exhaustive list of every single benefit one could attain. I have brainstormed and gathered my top 6 beneficial perks that would encourage someone to make the move over to working in software. As a friendly reminder do remember to take everything said here with a grain of salt and as my father would say, always do your own research even if you think something is true. Without further ado, feel free to read along and note that the pros identified below were based on experiences in the industry from the 2016 to the 2022 time frame, and a lot can change in one year, and so this was taken into account when describing the perks of the workforce.

High Demand

One of my favorite things about working in the software industry is the demand it currently has and growth for it, that is continuously shown. I was raised under the idea that I had to practically beg for work, regardless of what career I chose to pursue. After entering the industry, I discovered that when it came to software jobs, this could not have been any further from the truth. I am still amazed at the amount of messages I get every single day on LinkedIn alone from recruiters looking for candidates to interview with their clients or companies. It makes me feel like a celebrity or a well known public figure. All jokes aside, this does not at all mean that this is an easy industry to break into, actually quite the contrary. Without looking up data to back this claim up, just from my experience alone I have witnessed growth in the industry and see a high demand in companies that offer consulting services such as Accenture, Infosys, Capgemini, Cognizant and many more. I have also lived through companies expanding throughout the states, such as Apple breaking ground in their new Austin, Texas location in 2019. Or take for example companies like Deloitte, Tesla, Oracle, Snap, Indeed and even places like HEB, & Kroger which yes also offer software jobs, that have relocated to Texas alone during the time I've worked as an engineer. Company growth is not the only factor of a high rise for software jobs, but also the complexity of the system being built, among many other factors. One thing I've noticed is that, the longer or "more experience" you gain in the industry, the more desirable you seem to become to the companies out there. This makes sense as one starts to meet some of the ridiculous requirements placed in the job descriptions posted by these corporations. I'm talking about job descriptions I've seen in associate roles that have sentences like "must have a minimum 3 years experience in the industry ". When the only experience you have as a fresh graduate is a total of 1.5 years that was accumulated from an internship through your own university. No joke though, experience is gold for any company one chooses to interview for, as the years pass by the more demand you will be in as a software engineer from what I have seen, especially if you stick to one type of technology over those years as opposed to hopping around different skill sets in short periods of time.

Potential Travel

This may not be a perk to everyone, unless you are a person like me who loves to travel. Anyway, prior to the 2019 pandemic, I was working as a software consultant for a company called Infosys that required a lot of travel. As a consultant of an enterprise that offers consulting services such as Infosys, you are often mapped to a particular project when a client requires your particular area of expertise as a service for them. Meaning a company in need of a specific software service in this case a chatbot service for their website, would request such a service to this third party company and hence the group of folks with the required expertise are gathered and sent to work directly to the client's location which most of the time meant working out of town for me. At the time I was living in Indianapolis, Indiana, and though Indy had many corporations in need of software services within the city itself, most of our clients were from out of town. So that meant I got to travel back and forth for months or however long the duration of the project was set to be. Like I mentioned before, most of the clients we got were based out of town, so even if you made friends in the office, chances were that if they had a different skill set than you, they would end up in a different project than the one you were assigned. Anyway, I love to travel as mentioned before and was constantly sent back and forth between Indianapolis, Indiana and Dallas, Texas, before falling in love with my home state again and deciding to move to Texas leaving Indiana. Though I probably would have kept traveling had I stayed with the consulting firm, my decision to leave boiled down to two major reasons. One was location, I saw an opportunity to move back to Texas to be closer to my family and I took it. Second was pay, though not a humongous difference at the time the employer offered a higher salary than what I was getting, so I took the bait. Now if you are someone who treasures travel more than anything, you probably would not have made the same move I did and that is totally fine, especially when the company pays for your travel expenses even if it's just for work.

I will take this opportunity to note that most consulting firms work like this, or at least used to prior to the 2019 pandemic. I mean to say that they would take you as a consultant in their firm, as is, with the current skill set you possess. And based on that skill set, the consulting firm will ship you out to a client (company) that requires use of your skill set, for a specified duration of time. And usually in our case, we had the option of staying in that particular city or location for the duration of the project, or traveling back and forth to check on family etcetera. Note that I said consulting firms used to work like this, prior to the 2019 pandemic, as now talking to contractors and consultants at my current workplace, all of them instead of traveling are working remotely and have been since 2019. I don't know and, as they explained to me also don't know if this is going to change in the future or if they have simply be-come remote workers, for the rest of their employment at these firms. This is one of many areas in software affected by the pandemic that I will discuss in a later section, but I can verify that these consultants are working remotely. In the past two years that I have been with my current em-ployer as of 2020, I have yet to meet any of my current team-mates in person, whether at the actual work office or elsewhere, as they are scattered across the states.

That is not to say you still can't find a job in the soft-ware industry that will offer you travel, as I have heard from one of my 1 of my 3 friends working at Lockheed Martin, that since the pandemic has come to some sense of control he is back to traveling at least once a month. My other friend at Lockheed who is an accountant and not an engineer does not travel because his role does not require to do so and is currently working remotely. So, there is still hope even if a company decided to go fully remote, there are roles that may still require one to travel.

Remote Work

This is a great transition to the other elephant in the room as of 2022, and one of my favorite subjects to talk about, remote work. One of the major advantages of working in software as of 2022 is the opportunity for remote work, whether you like to travel or simply prefer to avoid the commute to an office every day, and or enjoy working from the comfort of your home. Again, one major positive outcome in the software industry and a resulting effect of the 2019 pandemic. Humans are social creatures, I understand, someone famous once said it and I can't remember who, but whether it is true or not I also understand that remote work is not for everyone.

This topic has become a topic of controversy for many reasons, one of which I will address is getting your actual work done. I've read many articles and news posts about CEOs and managers of corporations going against remote work, due to beliefs that employees tend to "pretend to work but not actually work" or "time being spent at work is difficult to manage". And if there is solid data to back this up, which I've not personally seen, then I understand and side with going against remote work. However, and I mean this in the most sincere way possible, speaking from experience, I find working from home to be much more productive than working in a traditional office setting. Reason being, I find people in the work office extremely distracting. Especially when they are having a meeting a few feet away from me with their headsets in the cubicles close to mine. To clarify, it's not just the people specifically that distract me but the all the input my ears receive from noises around my environment, that impede my concentration when working on a project or performing simple tasks like reading. The same reason I chose to read books at home instead of at a public Starbucks is the same reason I prefer to do my work at home, that being because my home is dead silent. I am a single guy that lives by himself without any pets or noise at home, and silence helps me concentrate extremely well since there is nothing interfering with my ears and eyes that would influence my ongoing cognitive processes. This is also how I used to study in college, at home locked into my room, as opposed to the college campus that was full of distractions, and this is also the same reason I work out at home versus working out at a public gym full of people. Even if I block audio input with some earphones, my eyesight usually still gets in my way, wanting to catch sight of everything that crosses its path. Working out with a blindfold and ears covered at a public gym seemed really impractical to me, so I decided to work out at home instead. Again because it is dead silent, and hence my productivity stays sharp, fun fact, this is probably a good explanation as to why I had to take many remedial reading courses all my life up to college. I simply could not read through the noisy environments I was placed in, so for me working remotely has helped me better achieve my tasks at work, no joke. I even got a raise this year, woohoo. Anyway, as I keep saying everyone is different, and I have met people that can dive deep into their tasks no matter how noisy it gets.

Another big advantage I personally see in remote work are the opportunities that have become available when finding work. I mean to say this opened doors for work opportunities in corporations or industries that are located outside of one's current residing city or country, or as we say in the industry "offshore". For example, weeks after Spotify had just announced that they had implemented a fully remote workplace, I had gotten a call from a recruiter of the company. She wanted to talk to me about a role she had to fill and of course she was smart to start by stating that the role was fully remote, so I listened. I ended up not interviewing with Spotify since my skill set was not what they were looking for, but the point is that this role was based out of The United Kingdom. Which I thought was awesome even though I was told I was not required to ever set foot in the UK offices since the role was remote, and that if for any unlikely reason they needed me at a spotty location they would send me to Austin, Texas not across the country. Traveling to a different country I guess would have been ideal for the travel junkie, but since we are talking about avoiding the office here and working remotely, this was super exciting news to hear.

Speaking of travel junkies, as of 2022 several "digital nomad visa" programs have emerged where you can travel across to different countries and work remotely in that country as long as you meet the requirements set by them. I've not done much digging, but if you are truly a fan of travel and remote work, this may be something worth investigating. From what I've gathered, most nomad programs require the applicant to meet some basic criteria in order to grant them permission to stay in their country and work remotely, for an extended period of time. These requirements tend to be things that are the following but not limited to: proving proof that you have remote work, make x of money per month, and have medical insurance among others. Another awesome opportunity emerged from the chaos of the 2019 pandemic, and something to think about if pursuing a career in software engineering working remotely.

With all that said, not all companies are adapting the fully remote model just yet, some employers are slowly progressing that way by offering a hybrid work model like my current employer. Ideally my employer wanted to go back to a full in office work model but realized how impractical that was given the pandemic situation and decided to change the policy to a 3 day in office work model with one way being "flexible". I've also heard and read articles of companies not wanting to adopt the remote model at all. I personally don't think it is a smart move from these enterprises, given how much money spent on leases they would probably save if they'd just get rid of some of their "office" space. As I stated earlier, though, I lack experience in entrepreneurship, so perhaps these companies have superb reasons for sticking to physical offices. Nonetheless, I think remote work is here to stay and not going anywhere especially for the software industry, I think the pandemic of 2019 simply sped up an inevitable trend.

Achievable Self Teaching Skills

Not all companies that hire software engineers, require you to have a degree. This statement is another controversial subject, but I have discovered it to be true. Of course, I am not just talking about the big dogs that make this possible in their enterprise, such as Google and Netflix or most if not all of FAANG (the 5 best performing technology companies). I simply want to make the public aware that it is still possible to break into the software industry without a degree in this field. There are many other companies like Shopify, LinkedIn, Airbnb and that offer opportunities to those with no degree, as long as you can prove you have what it takes to work in the industry. I am a huge advocate for education, but if you find a way to break into the industry without going the traditional route, by all means I encourage it, even if you plan on finishing school at the moment.

That said, the skills required to become a software engineer can most definitely be self-taught if you are good at self-teaching. Not to mention, there is an abundance of certifications one can take, to catch a company's eye. Want to work in development operations? Web development? Become a User experience designer? Database operator? You name it, there are endless programs you can get into, to get certified in your field of interest. This is very accessible in 20222, you are only a few google searches and clicks away from enrolling in a certification course or even just a learning course can come a long way. I have literally worked with people who did not have the software related degree, but most certainly possessed the skills to perform the job at hand. Some of these people came off as extremely talented at first glance, or extremely good problem solvers. Not to downplay the degree as it is extremely beneficial to have but if, say, you want to become a software engineer in "mobile application development", and you not only study hard enough but prove your skill set in that area. You actually develop mobile applications, be it for freelance or personal gain, then I can assure you, if you play your cards right, you will most certainly get noticed in this field. That said, keep in mind that you are competing against those that do have the degree, which oftentimes will probably take priority, unless they seem like an awful idea of a candidate, so always find a way to stand out and show the employer why you are a better candidate.

Let's change it up a bit and suppose the candidate does have a degree, but it is not in a related field of computer science or software. I had this one friend I met at my first software consulting job, who had a degree in accounting but was working as a fresh graduate in the same software consulting firm I was in. I of course asked him how and why he chose to work at the firm. His reasons as to why he preferred to be a software engineer instead of an accountant, which he worked 4 hard years to become, was simply because he wanted the higher pay. So he graduates and works at an accounting firm for the first year and then decides to break into tech right after. My brain was trying to figure out exactly how he accomplished all that? No certifications, no programming courses outside of work, nothing he instead said he practiced solving programming questions every day after work for at least one hour using the platform called Leetcode, which is very well known for that specific purpose. His technique was to dive right into the difficult questions and ignore the easy & medium tier questions Leetcode offers for practice. What was mesmerizing to me was, that not only was he able to use Leetcode to his advantage and break into software once, but he had done it a second time when he had decided to leave the software consulting firm for a higher paying role, breaking into a 6 figures as a software engineer at Capital One. From that moment on I became inspired by this guy and the transition he made from accounting to software engineering was remarkably impressive to say the least. Point is, that it can be done, the skills needed to break into tech can be attained through determination and self teachings.

One final note to bear in mind or rather something I overheard one time during my university studies back in 2015 as I passed by the database classroom was, "come on guys, you don't have to be good, just know the basics!" I took that without any context as the database instructor preached this at her class as I made my way to my own class, and it really stuck with me for some reason. Note that I did not have this professor as my database teacher, so I don't know her name, but I remembered this quote she yelled in her classroom randomly during my 3rd year working as a software engineer. "You don't have to be good, just know the basics", made me think about many different possible meanings to what she was trying to convey to her students, and at first I thought she was giving a pep talk to motivate her students to present their work on the white board, but no. It wasn't until years down the road I realized she was, actually trying to let the students know that they can worry about being proficient after the fact that they've landed the job. Which implied to me that the skills they needed to learn, will be learned when they need to cross that bridge, but also made me conclude that not everything will be taught by your university or certification program. So in essence, being a self-taught candidate can only work in one's favor when it comes to the software industry.

Transferable Skills

Once you have attained the desired skill set in the area of focus you want to work in, whether you are moving to a different company, just starting to break into tech, or getting promoted, the good news is that those skills you've attained will more than likely be transferable to whatever company or industry you decide to transition to. Unless, of course, you are making a drastic change in the industry and or branch of work that you are moving into. But generally, if you decide to for example study and get certified, or simply acquire years of experience on all there is to know about python programming, then you may be entitled to roles dealing with machine learning (artificial intelligence), web development, scripting and everything related to python programming where it is used as potential roles. This means, for example, that if for whatever reason you wish to transition from working with Uber technologies, to take that better offer twitter made you, with promises of better pay, benefits and your own personal tutor at your desk, you can do so comfortably if this next role is also a python related role, since you've already had the skill set for it.

Note again that this does not apply if you decide to make a drastic change in an engineering position or industry. For example, if you decide to make a change from let's say web development to maybe video game development, then keep in mind that the skills you have may not be all that transferable if you are specifically working on an area that has nothing to do with your skill set. Now of course there are many games out there that use machine learning, so if you're designing game tactics for a game company that requires machine learning then you are in luck as you already have the transferable skills for such a role through your knowledge of python. But say you were a python web developer before, and you got onboarded to a company such as DoorDash that demands you specifically to build an application that is meant for IOS only mobile devices (iPhones). Then in such cases the skills you possess, may not be directly transferable into an IOS software role which as of 2022, the last time I checked, still uses swift as their programming language and has not much to do with the python language.

Along with great compensation and benefits, often-times most companies I have seen, like to offer training or certifications sponsored by the very employers themselves. I think this is a great benefit to take advantage of, even if the program does not award you an actual certificate post completion. Nonetheless, this is great due to the fact that you are expanding your skill set, and more than likely those skills will be transferable within the software indus-try, wherever you choose to take your career. These train-ings from experience usually offer skill sets that are useful throughout most if not all the software careers of 2022 and on, I am talking about knowledge bases daily used in tech you may encounter at work such as of uses of the GitLab tool for source control versioning, or trainings I've had like full stack development in java and JavaScript programming languages for backend services. Thus, if an employer ever offers free or sponsored training, and or professional de-velopment, I recommend taking this opportunity wherever possible.

Salary Packages

Speaking of compensation and benefits, some people like me when I first started may be asking, well how much can I possibly make as a software engineer? Well as one of my college professors would often say "it depends' is usually a good answer". I remember one time I had a conversation with one of my friends in the industry who used to play football for the university we both graduated from, which is where we met. He was talking to me about how he had thought that pursuing a career in software would mean his salary would eventually make him a millionaire. That, this reason alone, was the reason he was comfortable leaving his dream to play professional football, as for him, it meant he'd be a millionaire either way. Now I am not saying this is not possible in any way, though realistically speaking the people I've seen become millionaires besides your already well established entrepreneurs, are people who end up starting successful software related enterprises. Generally as I'm sure I've heard somewhere "your 9-5" will not make you rich, in most cases I've seen at least. That said, I am also not trying to downplay the amount of pay you can attain as a software engineer. I started in the lower end of the spectrum my first few years working as a software engineer, but I had friends who jumped straight into a six-figure salary fresh out of graduation. They were able to achieve this either through solid connections in the industry, a serious amount of hard work, or both! My only objective at the time of graduation was to simply break into the industry, I was not concerned with whether or not my first employer was going to pay me in the 6-figure salary range or not as I figured I'd eventually move my way up there, which I ended up doing. But I will say, had I had the same mentality some of my friends did things might have ended up being a bit different for me, well maybe. However, no regrets here, I went the route I did as usually I like to take baby steps because when I take more than I can chew things don't end up working well or take much longer to get, but everyone is different, and my primary and sole objective at the time was to break into the industry. In any case, not all software related jobs from what I've seen start you off at that one hundred thousand plus salary a year, especially if you are an associate just starting out. Sometimes it's a little more than half of that, or in most cases most companies are willing to meet somewhere in between the 60-90 thousand mark as of 2022, keep in mind that cost of living and rate of pay as to what area you are going to work in, along with company budget are one of many factors that influence the offer corporations make you. Also know whom you are interviewing, if you are taking a role as a software engineer at a company that maybe does not depend heavily on software, like let's say someone like Home Depot. Then keep in mind that they may not be willing to negotiate their offer, but regardless always do your best to negotiate, you never know when it might work out for you! I've seen colleagues of mine ask for compensation way out of what a company's initial offering was and ended up getting what they asked for, so the moral of the story is that it doesn't hurt to try unless of course you are in desperate need of employment. Do note that when I say negotiate, I mean perform actual negotiation and not just simply demand more cash just because you desire it. In other words, if you say you are worth more than that is being offered just make sure you indeed know how much more you bring to the table before asking for a range, as more than likely questions will arise as to why you feel you deserve a higher pay than a person who is willing to do the same work for cheaper.

Back to the millionaire thing, there are companies that are extremely wealthy and are able to & willing to invest in a candidate that definitely seems worth their while. Some of these companies you may already know through the acronym FAANG or otherwise known as the "big five" tech companies to work for, and they are: Facebook, Apple, Amazon, Netflix and Google. Note that there are many other companies out there like these such as Microsoft, Blue Origin, Space-X, and tesla just to name a few, but to get my point across if you do well enough at the interviews at any of these companies which by the way are extremely intensive interview processes, then you can expect a great compensation reward as your salary pay. For example, last I checked on Glassdoor, and heard from a colleague that as of 202 and maybe even prior, Netflix supposedly pays their senior engineers around 300 thousand dollars a year. Again as said earlier take everything I say with a grain of salt and always do your own research, this number may change by the time you read this and don't forget to keep into account cost of living expenses. For instance, off the bat we generally know that California and New York are extremely expensive relative to other states in the United States, so maybe 300k a year in such places balances out to be about average? I don't actually know, I am just providing an example to base your research on. One other very important thing to note is that usually the companies that are willing to offer you these types of salaries have a very intensive and scrutinized interview process, I myself have witnessed! From my experience alone they will not only asses your soft and technical skills intensively for 8 hours a day 3 to 4 days straight, and have you speak to every manager, senior engineer and director possible in as much time as possible, but still at times have you come out with a presentation of your work experience in the industry. What I am trying to say in short is that, studying for any software related position in my experience is already an automatic requirement, so if you decide to interview with one of these tech giants be prepared to invest an unprecedented amount of time preparing for their questions. And if you have formed connections at these places, I recommend and encourage you to use them to your absolute advantage. Generally speaking, the higher the title or role usually the more pay, but note that this is not always the case. I have met full time associates that most times tend to have higher salary than regular software engineer contractors, or the other way around where a software contractor gets paid higher but has not paid leaves and or insurance, and doing the math sometimes the money does still play out to be more, but not again not always the case, so just something to look out for. Talking amongst peers we have also discovered that 2 or more engineers in the exact same position, for example 2 normal full time software engineers, can have an entirely different salary pay per year, and this is why I always encourage negotiation. Usually, the engineer that negotiated properly and or had more years of experience, is the one out of the two that has the higher salary pay. This also goes without saying, but always remember that usually higher pay comes with much higher responsibilities, and if you have found that to not be the case then consider yourself a lucky case.

Not everything has to be about money though and good healthcare packages, some employers like my current one are willing and able to offer you stock options as part of your compensation package. This is becoming extremely popular with startup companies but as I just mentioned there are plenty of other companies out there that do this and here are some honorable mentions, Verizon, HEB (grocery store), Microsoft and more. Though from what I gathered these stocks are not accessible until they "vest" meaning you are employed for a set period of time, they are a great addition to retirement aids like 401 k or pension plans, which I hear is or has already died down a bit. In addition to this, I have also worked with companies that are able to either reimburse or fully pay for continuing education, which could mean attaining your masters, PhD or maybe a second or first bachelor's degree. The only two catches here I've seen which I see as reasonable demands as opposed to a catch is that one, you of course pass your class otherwise you'll be forced to pay back the failed class, and second the degree you chose to pursue usually has to be related to the field in work you currently work in. I imagine the corporations usually do this so that you won't leave your current role for a different industry at a different corporation, but at the end of the day, all these benefits and terms vary by company.

THINGS TO CONSIDER IN A SOFTWARE CAREER

Like some careers I've seen there are demands a career in software often requires, it's not all sunshine and rainbows, especially if this field is not one that is enjoyed in the slightest. With that said, not every demand required from your field may actually be a drag but rather a fun pastime, again this all depends on the individual. Regardless, I will break down some of the most unexpected things I encountered in my career, and also some very much anticipated things I encountered while working.

Always a Student

My very first computer science professor told us once that it was literally impossible for someone to know all there is to know about a programming language the very first day of classes. After years of working in a computer science related field, this to me seems more and more increasingly true. There already is more than enough material to spend a lifetime learning a single technology like a programming language, and it doesn't help that new versions of that language and or new technologies emerge every six months to a year. Adding more stuff to learn about in the very field that is progressively growing, I mean there is literally a new iPhone release every new year to oversimplify things a notch.

Regardless, on my very first day working as a tech engineer, I had felt a bit overwhelmed due to the fact that I had never before worked in the field in a corporate professional setting. Also, not knowing the technology I was meant to work in for that employer at the time, being the PHP scripting language, made me panic even more. Of course, I had just broken into the industry so the last thing I wanted for myself was to blow the opportunity away, so I bought a PHP book, looked through the codebase day and night and even attempted to practice the language during my spare time. Now typically you have access to the internet, but I was working in a warehouse with barely any cellular connection miles away from civilization. If I wanted access to the internet I literally had to literally call the company's actual IT department in Kansas City to guide me through the hardware and software setup on their end and this took a couple of weeks to get right, and I had help from no one but the people on the phone with me. In other words, I was the IT and software department for this company, and I had much to learn, not knowing a thing about scripts and or networks when it came to the actual workforce. However, like most if not all employers I've had, this one also knew that I would need time to address the learning curve that came with the role I took and was more than happy to work with me, as he knew that what he needed was just a software engineer skilled enough to move the company forward. This was definitely not his first rodeo in hiring a software engineer, and I could tell that by the way he treated me. In the end, I eventually learned what I needed to learn and was able to perform whatever task assigned to me.

But the fear of not knowing whether I could get a particular task completed or not, never went away, and that is the point I am trying to make. I've been in this industry well over 5 years and still experience this type of doubt when a task with a new technology or something I've never touched before is assigned. But to this day, and this is not to brag because I know I am not the only one, I have not had a situation where I cannot learn what I have to get my work done. When working in this field, acknowledge that you will always be a student, but do not panic when an opportunity presents itself, where you are required to learn a new skill to perform your work, this happens more often than not, at least for me. Keep this especially in mind when you are jumping from one distinct role to another. I think this might have been covered before, but let's say you are jumping from a role where you had 2 years experience in working with the Java programming language onto a role that requires you to know the Go programming language. Or when you come from working as a database administrator onto mobile applications' developer, again 2 different roles that may not require the same skill set but as a software engineer you should be able to learn what is needed to solve related tasks, and so far I have seen this to be true both with myself and my peers. In other words, this is usually what opportunity looks like, sometimes it looks like something that is beneath you, I find this especially true when one is starting out. Other times it is the complete opposite, and one thing I've learned in life is that life does not wait for you to be ready. I mean to say that if you're waiting till the day you master a particular technology before you decide to start working on your software related job or personal project, then consider the possibility that that day may not come soon enough or at all. As I said in the beginning, most of these technologies have enough material for a human being to spend a lifetime learning all of its capabilities, so don't panic if you take on a role that requires a knowledge base you don't have at the moment and learn to adapt as you go.

The best thing an engineer can do in the field in my opinion is to learn to problem-solve and be as dynamic as possible, adapt as you need to and learn only what you need to for the task at hand. And this may be difficult for those truly passionate about tech, but try and avoid going down a rabbit hole of learning all there is to know about a particular technology that you will not use often or had just a little trouble with, as usually time is not that generous. I hear this from many motivational speakers and don't know if this is coincidence or not but speaking from my experience, if you are uncomfortable with a new position or task assigned to you that is usually a good sign. Meaning getting out of your comfort zone, and I will tweak this a bit as I don't always agree with these speakers, but usually getting out of the comfort zone is a good thing. Granted you are able to grow and successfully carry on whatever task assigned that made you uncomfortable in the first place, in other words being able to problem-solve in uncomfortable situations is more like it. By doing so, the skills required to solve a problem will be, either acquired or exercised during the solving process, which leads to growth on a personal and professional level. This will also help you discover on your own what you are capable of. I've had about two or three instances in my current role where I genuinely thought I would be let go of because of doubts I had in solving a particular problem that usually had a foreign technology I had to deal with. But as stated earlier, I focused on the baby steps and instead of spending hours learning an entire technology, I learned just enough pieces of code to carry on and solve my assigned tasks. This helps me be stress-free, which feels liberating to the point where I no longer panic or get imposter syndrome when I have to deal with technologies I don't know or never used before, because I am now confident enough to know that I will find a way to solve it or find an alternative if it cannot be solved as proposed. So in conclusion, when taking on software in general and not just as a corporate career take into account the fact that there will always be something to learn, regardless of the amount of experience one possesses in any area.

Interview Preparation

This is one of my biggest pet peeves for me personally, for many reasons, which I will get into. Interview preparation when interviewing for software engineering roles, nine times out of ten are a requirement. And I am specifically talking about two things in particular here when companies like to interview candidates, one is the technical round of the interview and the other is the problem-solving round of the interview, which by the way does get better over the years with one's experience. Notice that I said round for each, so before I dig into the weeds of these topics, I will describe a little bit of how some companies like to interview.

Most companies I have been with or interviewed like to break their interviews into stages, and each stage is broken down into different rounds of interviews about different topics. Once a candidate passes most or all of the stages of interviews, it is then when an offer is generated and presented to the candidate. Generally, a recruiter of some sort schedules a 30-minute call with the candidate, in which the recruiter gives information about the company and role they are looking to fill, and what they typically look for in a candidate. This time is also used for the candidate to give a brief overview about themselves and the areas of work they can be of service in, relative to what industries and technologies these candidates have worked in. If both the recruiter and candidate are a match and or the candidate expresses interest in the company or the role offered, the recruiter then schedules the first round or rounds of interviews. Many companies have adopted their own format of interviewing, but I am describing the general overview of how they like to do interviews for the most part.

The first stage of "interview" is usually a technical "assessment" or basically a technical exam on the skills "required" for the role to be interviewed. So for example, if you are interviewing for a "Python Developer" role, expect to have questions on this particular technology ranging from easy to difficult level. These assessments usually have a set timeframe in which you are to finish them, usually ranging from 75 to 90 minutes or more. These used to be in person exams but have now been take-home and fully online assessments as of 2019, in light of the pandemic of course. If you interview for a more generic or broader role, such as the title of software engineer, then expect questions more related to algorithmic problem-solving, and use of data structures for the technical take home assessment of the first stage. Again, these questions will range from level of difficulty starting in easy and working their way into more difficult questions. Depending on how the candidate does here, the company will make a decision as to whether or not to move on to the next stages of interviews with a particular candidate. Do note that some companies are much stricter than others when it comes to the passing grade required for these technical assessments within the first stage. For example, if you are interviewing for an associate role as you are just starting out, they may for example only expect you to attain a passing grade of somewhere between 60 and 70 percent in order to make it to the next rounds. The higher the role a candidate is interviewing for, then usually the higher the knowledge base required, which normally translates to a higher passing grade in these assessments. Note that there are also companies that are much stricter and may require a passing grade of 95% or more, regardless of what position a candidate is interviewing for. Additionally, in some cases the problems given at hand in these technical assessments, are sometimes not intended to be solved within the entire time frame given, and employers will make note of that prior to giving the candidate the assessment. In such cases, at times the employer analyzes the candidate's skill set by how the problem was approached rather than a grading system or its completion. When this tends to be the case, a senior engineer usually meets with the candidate online after the assessment is taken, so that the candidate can walk them through why and how the assessment problems were approached in the manner illustrated. Once this first stage is successfully completed, the next stage of interviews is set up by the recruiters, and these next 2 stages usually take up at least half or an entire day each.

Stage two, as I like to call it, consists of a five or six-hour day of pure interviews in which each interview round has one hour allocated to it. This second stage of interview questions usually contains topics about a candidate's experience in different work culture settings, behavioral analysis of the candidate, software design questions, team leadership skills questions, project retrospectives walk-throughs, and a final live coding technical challenge; this last one may be allocated for an hour and thirty minutes or more instead of one hour. These are topics I've seen company's cover but as I have mentioned before each company differs a little bit as to what topics or specific questions to ask the candidate about, one thing I can assure though is that that that last topic listed, final live coding technical challenge is one that will likely be used by any company that is looking to fill any software related role. This can translate to plenty of technical study and practice before deciding to interview with a company as you not only en-counter a technical assessment at the first stage but will most definitely display technical skills in a live setting at the second stage and sometimes the third stage as well. From experience this can be tedious and not to mention time-consuming as not only is there plenty of technical practice involved until the day of the interview, but as you can see the candidate more than likely will have to take time off just to go through another company's extensive

interview process, as these tend to be 6 hour long interviews. Do be conscious of the difficulty of the problems
presented at hand, but also note that when doing live interviews there is usually an interviewee and an "observer" at
the live session intended to act as your co-worker. Companies do this to see, of course how you work in a team,
so don't forget to think aloud and not hesitate to ask for
an opinion when having doubts as to how to implement a
solution for a problem. I am guilty of usually getting the
feeling of thinking everyone at the interview scene is there
to ask me trick questions and trick me into failing, but
usually it is the other way around, so keep that in mind
when interviewing. To sum it up, in this particular scenario
it is in the candidate's best interest to become comfortable
in walking someone else through the solution process, as it
will help interviewees assess the candidate's skill and areas
of strength. Other than that, areas where the interviewee
asks questions about team leadership and or behavioral
or company culture settings, are topics that one generally
tends to have good answers for due to the experiences acquired in their prior and current roles. For example, when
someone asks a question about how you dealt with a teammate that was hostile to you or someone else, simply talk
about a time when you encountered a hostile teammate
and how you and the team were able to come to a consensus at the end, and continue to work together effectively.
Maybe you gave this person their space until things cooled
off and then calmly and professionally, brought the team
together to reason as to what can be done from all parties

for the team to move forward and work cohesively, without any hostility. If you are a candidate who is just starting out or has maybe not yet encountered unprecedented conflicting scenarios at the workplace, simply talk about how you would go about solving an issue that presented itself. Nine out of ten times a candidate will likely deliver the answer an interviewee is looking for since all you really need is a bit of common sense and morality to answer these types of questions. Now if, like me, most of your experience involves introducing a feature on systems that were already designed and implemented from the ground up by teams other than the one you are in, the system design questions can feel a little bit tricky. I know they did for me, I was definitely caught off guard when I encountered an interview question that required me to design a whole system from the ground up for the duration of the hour allocated. I had never done it before at any of my roles and only during my university studies, which I did not remember as I had just encountered this question 5 years later already working as a software engineer. The only advice I can offer here is to pay attention to the engineers and higher up that are usually the one's in charge of doing this, learning how this is done at least at a high level will come in very handy not just for interviews but when working on a product, even if it is just a feature enhancement of some software. Also note that it is not as difficult as it sounds, for example when I got this question I was asked to design a retail store's website from the ground up, but once I got started I realized that I was talking about technology mechanisms that used on the day-to-day basis like databases, API calls, data structures, front ends back ends etcetera. Now, I know other complex systems exist, but If you can design a website service at a high level like this one, you can probably get away with designing almost anything. This made me realize that I was scared of system design questions not because of the complexity of the question asked but because I had never done it before, so it was more from fear of the unknown.

After both the first and second stage are successfully completed, usually comes the final round. This final round is another five to six-hour day process, but is mostly reserved for managers of different departments to come and interview the candidate. This is mostly done to determine which of the five or six departments the candidate would be the best fit for. Usually this is a decision made by the managers and some companies allow for the candidate to receive multiple offers from each respected department that wants to acquire said candidate, from which the candidate chooses one of those offers. This final round usually tends to be a day allocated to each manager presenting their department and what their team does for the company in regard to their specific domain or department. This tends to be a way of giving the candidate a glance as to what they could be potentially working in should they get hired for a specific domain. Sometimes the managers or directors conducting these interviews bring along a senior engineer from their team to assess the candidate's technical skills on the spot, so bear in mind that just because you made it to the final round, it does not mean you are done with the technicality of questions. That said, as a candidate of course always ask questions to make sure the company is a good fit for yourself, you also don't want to end up working in a toxic place or an environment you despise.

As far as what study material to take into account when studying for an interview, sometimes recruiters give you an outline as to what to expect for the day-long interviews. Oftentimes, though, I will note that these companies tend to ask questions on subjects I have not seen since college or have not used often at any of my roles as a software engineer. This could possibly be because I have branched out to an area of engineering that is more inclined to infra-structure setup and automation when it comes to software. Meaning setup of things like virtual servers, domains, and other cloud services for software to be able to run on. For this reason, I will say that it can be a little irritating when companies focus their technical interviews on very specific topics that you will not use very much at the role you are interviewing for. For example, since I've jumped into the industry back in 2016, I realized that companies have always loved to focus their technical questions heavily on "algorithm complexity" and or use of "complex data struc-tures". Which by the way I like, and I am all for it if the role at hand requires use of this knowledge extensively. But this can be painful study material if you have literally not used or seen this "data structure" material since col-lege, especially when you are in a role that rarely relies on such concepts or technologies. From experience, though, oftentimes not only are the interviews five times more difficult than the daily tasks the actual role requires, but they tend to focus on topics or skill sets that are rarely or ever used in the actual role at stake. I do notice this changing for the good though and as far as I can tell as of 2022 in my latest interview experience, companies seem to be asking questions more closely related to what actual technical skill set the role in question demands.

Do note that some corporations still use these topics to conduct their interviews but in some cases you will actually end up using these concepts, especially when interviewing for companies like the big five otherwise known as "FAANG", as introduced in the "Salary Packages" section of this book. These corporations actually rely heavily on these concepts and hence the reason why they have not changed their interview model, but that doesn't mean that there is only room for engineers with "algorithm and data structure knowledge" ; these are massive corporations with plenty of domains to interview for. Note that just like the big five, there are many other corporations out there that have a much tedious and radical interview process. So instead of a 3 stage interview expect something like a 5 or 6 stage interview process where each stage can take up to six hours or more of interview rounds. Sounds intense, I know, but don't be alarmed as for the most part, some of the companies that do this, tend to be worth the hassle. So if it is your dream to work at X company, I encourage you to interview with them regardless of what their process looks like.

The Double Standard

If I was CEO of a company I had started, and I was looking for skilled personnel to hire, I'd probably want to hire the workaholic that is passionate about his job over the person who would treat his position at my company as a "job" that pays the bills and nothing more doing just enough to keep their position. I understand this mindset coming from an entrepreneur, but again may I remind you that I am no entrepreneur as of yet. However, I also understand that people have a life of their own outside of work and not everyone's nine to five is their dream job or career. One thing I do want to talk about though is the double standard expectations I literally see at most companies I have interviewed for or encountered. I've had times during interviews where interviewees ask about any ongoing projects outside of work that are software related, and when I was first starting off I did have some because again I had no prior relevant work experience. A couple of years down the road though, and I don't know if this is just me getting older, but the last thing I wanted to do after my work shift was open another laptop again and glare at that screen until the day concluded. There are other hobbies and things I enjoy doing outside of work, not to mention how unhealthy it probably is for anyone's eyesight to be glued to a laptop for the remainder of the day, outside of work hours in which this is done all shift. The forty-hour work week is enough for me to log off and want to do literally anything that does not feel like work after work, which usually translates to working on a completely different passion, having a little fun or simply resting if it was a hectic day. Now nothing against those working on a software related passion project outside of work hours, but this is definitely not something I currently do as the forty-hour week for me tends to usually be enough. I don't eat, breathe and sleep software as companies tend to expect to see when digging into my hobbies and interests. I will say though that If I did have such a passion project, I probably would have instead gone the entrepreneur route and at least attempted creating a start-up of my own. Realistically if this was the goal from the beginning, I probably would have lacked the funding to do so. And in such a case, this scenario for me would justify working on such a software project outside of work hours. I know a few friends who have gone this route and hence the reason they are not working for someone else, making someone else's software as their own keeps them more than plenty busy most days of their week. Though again, as I have repeated from the very beginning though I personally don't currently possess any entrepreneur experience as of the writing of this book, 2022. Also, I wanted to bring this topic up to let you the reader know that there is still room in this industry for guys like us. Though companies constantly look for the double standard as to what other software projects a candidate touches outside of work, this usually is not a strict requirement for them.

I don't mean to say that software is not my passion, but it is one of my many interests in life, after all I put myself through four years of college for a career in it willingly. That said, when I am asked about such things I respond with honesty without being rude and let the interviewer know that I still love what I do, as it took me four years to break into the industry alone. If that does not show dedication and determination I don't know what does, I then proceed to walk them through my actual hobbies, passion projects and life outside of software if that is genuinely what they were interested in knowing in the first place, which is rare but has happened. And yes writing is a hobby of mine hence the creation of this book and no I did not conveniently make the book software related, to meet the double standard I genuinely always wanted to have a book of my own published to the world. Bottom line, the message that I am trying to convey here is to be honest about your hobbies and passion projects when asked about in an interview, and never be afraid to tell the truth about what it is you love doing outside of work if it is not software related. As crazy as it may seem, most companies worth working for understand that candidates have lives and families to attend to outside of their software jobs, so never be afraid to admit that you have not or do not work on software projects outside of work.

The Importance of Soft Skills

One of the most underrated skills I personally see people often lack in this industry are people skills and soft skills. I have worked with many people who have been in a position that requires managerial and or well versed communication skills, to fulfill their job, and lack the experience to do so. I notice this to be a trend because of the promotion system that corporations usually tend to have in place with their employees. Meaning to say that an engineer at times tends to be promoted to a leadership or managerial role such as a technical lead and or software manager, which usually involves dealing constantly with people under them and above them. However, the promotion is most likely granted because the candidate has either exceeded the salary range limit of their current role or because they tend to do really well in performance when it comes to their current role, which usually is a mostly technical role. I am not saying soft skills are not a thing for a software engineer they most certainly are, as nine out of ten times these engineers work in teams, but I am saying that a transition from an engineer to a manager can be catastrophic for the employee and the people under them. I find this to be generally true if they lack the soft skills of high demand for such roles. Though these promotions may work in the favor of the employee, if moving up the ranks, this is how "bosses", not leaders, and a toxic workplace is born. I'm talking about managers that demand dangerously tight deadlines and are constantly asking for their employees to work overtime, with little to no break time in between projects. These tight deadlines usually arise because of the fact that these software of program managers have already made promises to their higher up or as corporate likes to call them their "skip level", to deliver x amount of projects by some ridiculous unrealistic date, either to impress the higher ups in their newly acquainted role, or simply because they don't know how to negotiate with their superiors. This can also occur when such managers become intimidated by their superiors and accept whatever deadline is requested from them, regardless of whether or not such a project is feasible within the given deadline. When these decisions are made without first consulting the actual team that is to physically and mentally work on a set project, the work environment can become stressful, unpleasant and discouraging. Not to mention, the team under such a manager is not the only one that is going to suffer, but the manager also tends to look very bad to the people they report to, when set deadlines are pushed further and not met.

This can be a common issue with new teams and or new management, and I have lived through this scenario myself. This can also be common with "newly" built teams that have not had the experience of working enough within themselves to come up with a consensus as to how to estimate, commit and deliver a project at hand. When I say teams, I don't just mean the software development team that actually gets their hands dirty making the product, but the people these teams work with directly or indirectly. People like the product owners, project, software managers and team leads just to name a few. When a manager is taking on a project presented to them by their superiors, they should not only have their software development team present, to determine the feasibility and estimated delivery of a project, but anyone else that they may need input from. Therefore, if such a manager is unable to explain the technical complexities to their higher ups that may be the cause of set projects not being possible, the development team can jump in and help in this area. Additionally, in talking to the software development team about proposed projects live, both the manager and their superiors can better understand what projects can be completed by what deadlines and more importantly why those decisions are made the way they are. This will also help address dependencies or missing components dependent on another team that need to be addressed before even considering taking on a project, and managers may not always be aware of those dependencies at first hand. This is why it is very important to not be intimidated by the higher ups of a corporation and be able to explain to them in the simplest terms the technicalities or reasons as to why specific projects can or cannot be completed within proposed deadlines. Failure to do so will most likely backfire on the managers and their downstream teams not speaking up more than anyone. Learning to reason with people or a higher up as to why something or not can be done by a suggested deadline comes a long way, and the effects of that outcome will always domino down the streams to the people a manager reports to, for example. If I learned anything in regard to soft skills, it is that teamwork, communication, time management and adaptability are of the most crucial skills to possess at all levels. From the software engineering teams all the way up to the project managers, software managers, directors, vice presidents and any other roles that come after that.

As mentioned before these are crucial skills at all levels, and to stop picking on the principal engineers and managers, I will note that I have also witnessed, and I'm guilty of, at times lacking these skills as a software engineer. And not to justify the lack of soft skills but speaking for myself, I have always considered myself an extremely reserved person and most of the time only speak when I am required to do so. Being in the industry for a while though, I notice that this tends to be a default personality type for many engineers, that at least from my experience may not be of best interest. I am not suggesting one changes their personality to get their job done, but I am saying that if an individual as an engineer does not feel something is right within their team be it because of an unrealistic deadline, external dependency, lack of materials to complete a project or literally anything else of concern that may jeopardize the team's integrity or wellbeing, they should always speak up. The team will not suffer but rather benefit from this and be attentive in realizing the risks identified by the member who chose to speak up. As mentioned before, I have worked in a toxic environment, where unrealistic deadlines and commitments to projects were made without prompting the development team for any feedback, whatsoever. From such experiences, I can say that in the beginning I had chosen to remain silent as to what risks and unrealistic commitments I saw in the projects assigned to my team. This was done out of fear simply because I was very intimidated at my superiors which were specifically my assigned principal engineer lead, project and software managers, and also I was just hired to work in this "newly formed team", so I did not want to come off as the entitled millennial that is difficult to work with. The third reason I had chosen not to speak up was because I genuinely thought we would somehow get through the unrealistic projects and dates assigned, and I say this because I would never see a single team member ever speak up, when we got these projects allocated to us until the very last minute when the project was due. This last reason really got to me, because not witnessing anyone ever speak up when we spontaneously got a new impracticable project assigned out of thin air made me think of three possibilities as to why this was the case. The first and best case scenario that I came up with in my mind was that I was placed in a team of super talented engineers of a whole other level, and that I was probably the weakest link in the team, since I felt I was the only one that always had concerns or saw red flags in the projects being assigned. I thought to myself "well no one is speaking up, my team-mates are probably not worried in the slightest because they are likely extremely good at what they do". So then I decided to keep my questions to myself and collaborate intensively with my teammates, and address whatever project related questions I had with them instead, as they probably had much to teach me if I was the only one with concerns in my brain. Then a second and most likely scenario came to mind which was the possibility that my teammates were just as intimidated if not more by our managers and principal engineer leads demands, that chose to also remain silent as opposed to risking upsetting them and therefore chose to let things be. The last, and perhaps most catastrophic scenario possible that came to me, was that my teammates did not have any clue in the slightest as to what effort, dependencies and or technology stack the projects assigned to us had involved. So there was no way for them to actually know whether the given projects were feasible or not in the first place with the tight deadlines set. I came to the conclusion that my teammates trusted the managers and people who assigned a project to our team, to have had a well established knowledge base, to have allocated a reasonable time frame and resources required for the assigned project at hand to be completed. So to sum it up in my opinion, they decided not to speak up, and question the tasks at hand as opposed to potentially coming off as ignorant, since again we were a "newly" built team after all. After becoming very well acquainted with my teammates, I realized that they were not speaking up due to a combination of scenarios two and three, and not because of best case scenario, scenario one. As you can guess, this resulted in constant overtime work, pushing deadlines month after month for 4 months straight, and literally only completing one out of four projects assigned in time until the team finally decided to speak up. By team, I mean the actual team and not just me speaking up, taking matters directly to our manager, and director addressing the hostile work environment that had emerged, and our explanation as to why no project is ever completed. We finally spoke up about the toxic work environment that had been growing and proposed we follow a more organized way of working as opposed to ad hoc to get things on track. Then things slowly improved for the better after that as we finally started implementing "scrum principles" (google time if you are not familiar with this term) when performing our work as opposed to just playing everything by ear or as "needed". Note that though this was a negative experience for me and my team, it was a learning experience and this goes to show that it wasn't all the fault of the people at the top or "higher ups" that caused the birth of a chaotic birthplace. The development team lacked the proper people and communication skills and comfort to raise concerns over the projects assigned and took the assignments in without any doubt or question whatsoever.

For this reason, team bonding activities are very common within the engineering industry as I have seen many times, but the fact that we were hired during a pandemic event may have been the reason many traditional onboarding processes and activities like these may have been skipped. Note that there will also be times where an engineer may be placed in a team that does not exactly get along, and that is totally ok. I have also witnessed such a scenario at one of my previous employers and can say that such teams can still find common ground and work together. In simplest terms, not everyone that is placed in the same team is your friend nor are they obligated to be under any circumstances to work together. Back in the 2019 pre-pandemic, I was placed in a team of people who shared a common knowledge base or experience in relation to "modern" web development, as we were to perform work related to back-end and front end relative to the web development technology. The point is there was this particular team member that frequently got in a heated argument with our technology lead when it came to the design of the product or in this case web application proof of concept that we were tasked with designing and implementing as part of our assigned project. Each presenting their valid reasons as to why their design was the better match, they could never come to an agreement as to which actually was better. This intrigued me as I was an "inferior" engineer compared to them at the time since I had just started to move up in the industry, while they were veterans, so I really looked up to them. That aside though, our tech lead proposed a solution and this for me was the demonstration of good people skills, but he proposed the team tries his design first, and if the team is not pleased with it, to then have the team try-out, my other teammate's proposed solution. My teammate, the senior engineer that was arguing against the lead's proposed design finally said "Ok, fine, I don't agree with it, but we need to get moving, or we'll never get started so fine, I agree to implement this design but know that I don't agree with it". Those were the words of my colleague, which just blew my mind, because even though he strongly disagreed with our team's lead design, he agreed to implement it and they both found common ground to move the team and the project forward. From that point on we all worked collaboratively and finished the proposed design from my tech lead, and at that moment I realized that a good team is one that is willing and able to work as a cohesive unit. I always used to think teamwork implied getting along with each other and or possibly becoming friends to work as a unit, but that day my colleague taught me otherwise. I eventually became friends with this person, and he later admitted to me that he did not like most people in the team, just as a side note that blew my mind even more as he worked flawlessly as an effective team member with us every single day. Nonetheless, I don't mean to sound like a broken record, but I hope the sharing of these experiences and observations I have had in the workforce help demonstrate the importance of soft skills in the industry, or just life in general for that matter.

Work-Life Balance

From experience, I can say the work-life balance of a software engineer can truly vary, and as a general rule of thumb I think this goes without saying, but if you are working for a startup, changes are your work life, is also just your everyday life. Now usually that comes with higher compensation, but fewer benefits or sometimes more benefits, it all just depends on the company and its funding. Note that these enterprises can also be much more volatile as opposed to companies that have been around since the very beginning of the start of the technology era. As I have mentioned before, I am not much of an entrepreneur and I dare say I have yet to work at a startup but will most likely avoid it if I can, unless I was in need of immediate employ-ment. I was taught to avoid as much risk as possible when I can and therefore the fear of relatively volatile enterprises, even if the pay tends to be generous, which of course it is usually because well, work life balance. I might give it a try one of these days though, as I do hear friends getting some crazy deals, that said though it is not just startups that can take up a good portion of one's work-life balance. Compa-nies that have been around for years and are considered relatively more stable can also eat up one's personal time, and this I do say from experience.

At my current employer, for example, a year after work-ing with them things started to get a little hectic as the deadline to our project approached. There were multiple weeks where I had to work weekends, not because anyone had asked me to, but because the amount of work I had simply spilled over to Saturdays and sometimes Sundays. There were also multiple occasions where I had to work 12 to 16-hour shifts, to either correct a mistake in our project or just meet the deadline my team and I had committed to, and no this was not the toxic workplace I had de-scribed earlier this was a totally different employer, things were actually great with this employer. This was temporary though as it only lasted two to three months at most and the rest of the time I have been there, has been a complete shift to an amazing work-life balance. I want to note that more than likely there will come a time like this at every employer one decides to work in, whether it is a startup or not. Because I literally have experienced times where I am simply required not asked but required to put in extra hours and effort of work to catch up on my tasks be it due to meetings in the way or simply the amount of work I get assigned. That said everything usually ends up balancing itself and the rest of the months that I am not stacked I tend to have more than enough time to complete the tasks assigned to me, I even had way too much free time at one point with my 2019 employer that I decided to make the move to a different company, and they even offered me double what I made to take their offer. Anyway, at the time with my 2019 employer, the tasks assigned to my team were extremely trivial, so much so that the rest of the time at work was time given to us to work on personal projects and or focusing on learning a new "skill" as our bosses would say to us. The amount of free time was so abundant that nothing could beat boredom anymore, we didn't want to go home in case they needed us during work hours, and so they never did, so we ended up getting paid to literally stand by until needed, which the day never came. At that point, my now employer as of 2020 had contacted me via linked, and asked if I wanted to interview with them. I said yes in a heartbeat and not because of the salary range that the recruiter had mentioned to me but because of the projects they had going on. The urge for me to do something other than "learn something on my own" to stand by until needed, was greater than ever, after all as I mentioned in the beginning I had put myself through years in school to actually work on something software related. So after interviewing with this company, everything turned out for the better, and they literally made me an offer I just could not refuse. I'm not just referring to the compensation and benefits though they did double my salary and had me transition from contractor to now full time employee at their company, but I was genuinely excited to do any form of work with this new employer. My days of feeling like a benched seventh string football player were over, and to this day I have stuck through the ups and downs with this employer, as they have been the best corporation I have ever worked in thus far. The moral of this story is, as a wise man once told me, too much of anything can be bad for you. My father's sayings weren't always the best or the most accurate, but this one is a personal favorite of mine.

Some things to note when looking for work are job descriptions with things like "on call support, or production deployment offshore support". Yes this can imply that work-life balance may not be of the best quality when you see this in job descriptions from corporations, but know that, this may not necessarily be the case. This can sometimes simply mean that as opposed to working a traditional nine to five, your 9 to 5 is shifted to a 10 to 6 hour schedule or maybe evening hours if they mention "offshore". So don't be alarmed, for example in my particular case with my current employer, where you have "occasional" customer support, it isn't as bad as it sounds. This usually means being on call while at your traditional nine to five or being on call even after work hours, but only for catastrophic incidents, which has been only about 2 or 3 times in the 2.5 years I have been with this company. One perk to being called for work after an employee's normal work hours is that, whatever hours the employee worked apart from their regular shift hours, those are simply subtracted from the normal weekly schedule. This is done in order to avoid working overtime, as this is usually not allowed unless approved by the manager. These are some things to consider that may vary by company depending on where you work, this is just an explanation of my current situation at my workplace. That said, if you are hoping to look for enterprises that will pay you to sit in a bench, until your attention is needed, know that such companies exist, but if like me, you fear losing your professional skill set, this may not be in your best interest.

Uninterrupted Work Time

Meetings Meetings Meetings, this used to be a frequent problem with every employer I would set foot in, a meeting was requested for just about any topic or question regardless of how small it was. As much as I hate slack when it comes to such instances, I want to say thank goodness for slack skype messenger and literally any other platform I have used at work to sort out the little things. Oftentimes, ninety percent of the meetings I would join did not require my attention and or had little to nothing to do with me. This would cause several issues especially when first starting out, causing me to fall behind on my work and work after hours to simply catch up on my tasks but not necessarily because I was overloaded. I understand that there are meetings to simply keep one in the loop as to the direction the company or team domain is going so that no one is lost when changes go into effect, or meeting setups for daily status updates on projects. However, I was frequently included in many meetings where the lead or manager's presence was needed but not the developers themselves, and though I understand this can be a good learning experience as to what the future holds for those that aspire to move up the corporate ladder. Everyone in the team usually has more than enough to chew from when it comes to work load, in the end I discovered that I was not required to join such meetings and can proudly say that I know to decline every meeting that can be solved with a simple Slack messaging conversation, or any meeting I have no business in being in to which my presence will add no value. Of Course, I advise anyone to discuss the situation with their manager or higher up before taking actions like I have, as there may actually be valid reasons to which an employee may be included in such meetings. Time management is extremely important and therefore the reason I advise against wasting time in meetings, one does not need to be in if it can be avoided.

That said, I will take this chance to talk about status update meetings that work models like the "scrum" methodology tend to use. In the scrum way of creating software there are a set of meetings that take place during specific time frames, for example work is usually done in the form of "sprints" or 10 work days, in my employer's case. Every day that the sprint is in session, there exists a meeting at the start of the day that is reserved for updates on what each individual engineer is working on. In these meetings each engineer gives the update on where they are on their assigned project tasks and what impediments they are currently facing, this is meant to be a conversation between team members to help each other progress. Depending on how big a team is, the meeting is not supposed to exceed a maximum of 30 minutes every day, but again this also depends on how big a team is as I have worked in extremely large teams. Typically, these meetings are called "stand-up" meetings, and are to be held in a stand-up position as opposed to sitting down, the reason being is that standing up is more unpleasant and hence should prompt the person giving the update to be quick and effective when giving their updates. However, this rule was constantly violated during my experience working with a "newly" developed team at one of my employers, and it was frustrating because these thirty-minute sessions turned into 2 hour long meetings every single day. I am not exaggerating here, I said 2 hours, and I eventually came to notice that the reason these meetings ran for much longer than needed was because certain teammates had never before worked in scrum stand-up sessions. These members were both our senior and technical lead engineers, which were usually in charge and did not take feedback well from employees with a lower title on the screen. What was happening was that, every time one of these engineers shouted out their update, they had decided to turn the meeting session into their own personal troubleshooting livestream, to address whatever workload they had assigned for that day. Again teammates attempted at speaking up against what was happening here, and these engineers listened for one or 2 days at most, but continued to turn the daily standup meeting into their troubleshooting session meeting for months and months until again teammates finally decided to speak about this in retrospective sessions and meetings with the direct manager, which ended up solving the problem. Everyone works differently, and this just displayed how these two fellow engineers were so used to working in a particular meeting setting for the rest of their day with people of all kinds on board. Which from my observation was not really their fault as they have worked in such un-organized settings for many years, so this was surprisingly the first time that they were proposed to work in an "agile" setting through the use of "scrum" methodologies. At any rate, like these folks, anyone can adapt to modern work settings and whether these settings work or not, I urge everyone to take into account efficient time management to not only complete one's own work but allow others to perform their tasks as well. Uninterrupted work time can really level out the battlefield when it comes to work-life balance, so I make sure to only attend meetings where I am truly needed and always verify that my own time is always respected, as I am willing to respect others' time.

High Competition

Though this is a field of high demand, there is also usually plenty of other fish in the sea from which companies can choose to hire. Just another thing to keep in mind when presenting your resume or linked in profile to a potential employer. This, like many markets out there, can feel like a very saturated market, the best case scenario to breaking into the industry in my opinion are probably mass hiring events that some corporations tend to have. These are great for people who have a general knowledge base and or enough experience in the industry at the beginner level, as the company will more than likely still have room for "fresh" candidates at one of their mass hiring events. This does not mean it is impossible to get hired through more traditional or other means, as I have mentioned before, recruiters tend to be the ones to reach out from time to time looking for candidates to join their client's company. Still, I would not recommend waiting around to be discovered, and therefore I encourage submitting as many applications as possible to as many employers as possible, as a Google recruiter once told me.

Because even though engineers tend to be in high demand, the chances of actually getting hired at an enterprise tend to vary per company. In other words, just because you did "great" at a corporation's enterprise, it does not mean that you have secured the position, I'd say this is only true when you have an offer letter in your presence. From experience, I remember being told at least three times from three different employers that I have done great in all the rounds of their interviews and yet not a single one of them had decided to move forward with me. When asked about reasons why I got, responses related to other candidates having more years of experience, or having an even better solution to a problem I was asked to solve during one of their interviews. This made me realize that though recruiters are actively reaching out, at the end of the day what matters most is how close of a match a candidate is to what the corporations are looking for. In short, corporations can be extremely picky and kind words like "you're doing great" or "you seem like the perfect candidate" mean nothing, until the offer letter is presented at hand. There can also be instances where it is not necessarily someone better than you that was acquired for the role of interest, but it may be the case where a company decided to go with a candidate with the same skill set as you, that is willing to work for much less. Yes, there are corporations that are willing to invest in the employees they hire and pay what they feel they are worth if these candidates can prove themselves. However, at the end of the day we must remember that any existing and operating enterprise out there is looking to make some sort of revenue within their business, they are in the business industry, and whatever measures they have to take to keep the business alive and blooming, those measures will be exercised without a second thought. Sometimes this means layoffs, or as described in this case hiring people with the same skill set willing to work for cheap. Never bring down your value though if this tends to be the case as someone has something they can usually bring to the table, and if you know what you're worth and can do for an enterprise, then stand by your ground and evaluate yourself accordingly, but of course be willing to prove what you say you can do that is what negotiation is.

Always doing your own due diligence when interviewing or negotiating is a no-brainer, and with such high competition come unexpected scenarios as to why you did not get the role after passing every stage of interviews set by the interviewee. So in such scenarios like employers taking on candidates that simply had more experience in the game, there is not much one can do there. But if, say, they took a candidate who came up with a much better solution to the problem, then as an engineer one should know that they need to practice their problem-solving skills a little more. In simplest terms, there always exists someone who is more proficient or, as the saying goes, "better" at the thing one is trying to do, and it is our job as engineers to do everything in our power to become that "better or more skilled" candidate.

BREAKING INTO THE INDUSTRY

There are many paths a person can take when wanting to break into the software industry, I have met all kinds of people throughout my life. I have witnessed colleagues and friends that had it relatively "easy" when making it to the software workforce compared to other professionals. I have witnessed the power that connections with people in the industry can do for a person, but have also lived through the challenges one can encounter when attempting to break into this field. Irrespective of where one might be in the process of breaking into the software industry, I will take this opportunity to talk about things that may or may not be common knowledge, things I personally felt I had to do to get noticed and other methods I saw my friends and colleagues used to break into the field of engineering. The only thing I wish to highlight here is that everyone's route can and will be different, and this is by no means a guide to breaking into the field of software engineering.

Things You May or May Not Know

Some of these topics may already be common knowledge to some people, or may be new and perhaps useful information for candidates looking into taking on an engineering career. I used to think the quickest and safest way to break into any industry was to simply go to school for that particular subject. And I did so, thinking that with the simple fact that I had earned a degree in a particular field, that I was entitled to work in the field of interest. Though luckily years before graduation, after talking to many colleagues in the industry and graduates I realized that there were many more variables to take into account. It was then when I realized that the bachelor's degree from the university I attended was not necessarily a guaranteed ticket to the industry I was attempting to break into. Employers want to see what it is you have accomplished in the industry, before proceeding to screening you, so this to me meant that I had to attain some sort of experience prior to graduation to supplement the degree acquired at hand. I again had no clue how to accomplish this, since I had originally thought the career came magically after attaining the degree. During a professional development class, I discovered what the word internship meant, and saw an opportunity for a head start in working in the software business. I found out that it was through an internship where my chances were best at getting hired for a software engineering role, since I had no related experience in the field at the time.

After finally landing an interview through my school's website, and doing well displaying my acquired problem-solving skills from the couple of years of practice I had at the university, I had become a new intern as a software engineer, at a company focused on tile production and distribution. I know, this did not sound like the ideal job for tech, and I was genuinely surprised that a tile production company had openings for software interns. After a week of working there though I had discovered that what they needed was not only an in person software team but an IT department at the facility, but the title read Internship to probably justify the pay offered through that internship which to me read cost savings. Regardless, all this was irrelevant to me and I could not help but feel joyful and proud to have landed my first internship ever, as it now meant I could add some related work experience to supplement my degree once attained. A year later, I acquired my second internship and sometime in between that time up to graduation I had my first freelance project to add to my experience on my resume. In other words, as I already described in prior sections, I recognized that I was just a number when it came to candidate fishing, and I had to find a way to stand out among the pond of fish that also had acquired their degree as I had. This was my way of standing out and the moral of the story is to always do your own research, again had I never talked to any graduates or guest speakers at my school that were already in the industry, I probably would have taken much longer to break into the software engineering industry. I was fortunate enough to be able to meet people that were already in the workforce that could offer me a glimpse as to what life looked like after graduation, prompting me to take action in whatever way possible to gain software related experience prior to graduation. Now of course there are companies out there that are so picky that they refuse to count internships as actual experience for fresh graduates for whatever reason. I have heard about this and seen it written on job descriptions on LinkedIn, but I cannot confirm as to whether this is a thing or not, as I have personally not experienced it myself. But the companies I have worked for have considered all parts of my experience prior to graduation actual experience, and I am referring to internships, freelance work or other volunteer work. I found this to be especially true when one is starting out as a fresh graduate. I think these experiences are good tools to have under one's sleeves when one is starting to break into corporate. I remember interviewing for my first full time job a week after graduation to start as an associate software consultant, and the interviewees having me walk them through my internship experience and talk about the freelance project I had completed for a "client" of mine who had her own business and needed a website for her services. They focused more intensively on the freelance project and IOS application I had completed at one of the internship programs, than they did on my actual internship experience. So much so that they had me demonstrate these two projects live, to see the outcome of my engineering practices put into place. Though this made sense as the position I was interviewing for was "project based" and required me to make software projects similar to what I had showcased for the company's internal clients once I got hired. This was least expected on my end since it was constantly stressed in my brain that most employers wanted to see experience even if the candidate is a fresh graduate. But then again due to the nature of the work I ended up doing this made complete sense, and in the end I was still asked about my experiences at these internships so that validation for the experience was still present. As stated previously, corporations also focus on one of the most important aspects being, what was actually done with the skill set an individual claims to possess and if it can be demonstrated. Meaning to say that even technical coding questions were thrown onto me when I interviewed for my first full time engineering role, along with all the other elements I have described in the interview process companies like to follow.

At any rate, this goes to show how ignorant I was, when it came to breaking into the industry. Like some people I know, if I had not done the digging and just focused on attaining the degree while working at the hospital warehouse I was at, I might not have made it into the software industry directly after graduation. That said, there are many other routes I've seen people take in order to break into the industry, and one of them covers not having any related experience in the engineering field prior to graduation. So, I mean to say that even though the people that did not do the digging to jump into the field immediately, eventually broke in and some of them got a much better compensation package than I did when I broke into the industry. These are just a couple of routes I have seen taken, but I will cover these in a later section and steps that were taken by either peers or myself to work in the field of software. In short, I think the message here is quite clear, and working hard as part of a process to break into any industry is a given and implied in any goal that one sets for themselves. It happens frequently where motivational speakers shout out that one must work hard but fail to get into the specifics of what that effort specifically looks like. For that reason, instead of telling the reader to simply work hard in one sentence, to break into the field. I decided to focus on the specifics of what I thought was needed to break into the field that was not exactly common knowledge to me but could be considered as such.

Do what You Must

One thing I have learned in life is that there are usually sacrifices to make when it comes to pursuing a goal or dream one sets their mind to. Sometimes there are sacrifices that one may not want to make and or try to avoid if possible. Other times these sacrifices may not be a big deal or even something totally comfortable doing. During my university studies, as I may have already mentioned before, I had always struggled with reading and math courses. I recognize how ironic this can sound, but it is true, taking on college level courses only made things a bit more difficult for me, but in the end I knew that I simply needed more study time and practice than other students. The point I am trying to make here is that in order to reach my goal of graduating with a computer science degree, there was some serious time management that needed to be done on my end. I soon realized that 2 hours spent at the gym on a five-day basis with full time work and full time university enrollment was something that had to be cut down to 45 minutes a day 3 days a week instead. Also, the weekend getaways with friends and or Sunday nights with family had to be brought down to a minimum at times to make an extra effort of studying for final exams. Lastly, not to make excuses, but full time work with full time university enrollment not only kept me busy seven days a week but was also the root cause of me flunking a couple of courses during intense mini mester sessions. Turns out that even drinking enough caffeine to revive not one but two elephants, the day of the final exam, hoping to score a home run, in order to outweigh my mediocre class performance, never did me any favors. Now I know I will probably get a lot of backlash here, as there is always someone out there that can and has juggled it all in the past, being able to handle both work, school and even raising a child all at once. I get it, people out there like this do exist, I am not saying they don't, I believe it, and I am forever amazed and jealous at the talent of these people. This simply was not the case for me, as every attempt in doing so resulted in free money donations to the university I attended. Meaning to say that, I had to retake every failed class again and again, until I tried a different method that ended up working for myself. Turns out all I had to do was cut my work hours in half, and use the additional time I had spent working as study practice, and or recovery. Yes, I say recovery as I had noticed that every time I would take a test when also having a full time job, I would end up taking the exam in a state of exhaustion. So I really mean it when I say the caffeine did nothing for me. I remember it like it was yesterday, when taking an exam being extremely tired fighting sleep, I was also fighting my own reasoning perception and could not make sense of the questions being asked in my exam. This was both due to lack of study time which was a result of lack of sleep from going straight into work after class, without time to actually digest the lectures talked about and much less actually having spare time to study. You're probably thinking, well, why not study at work? Yeah, tried that, but the idle time at work that did present itself was not only a very narrow window, but extremely scarce on any given day, I mean I did work at a healthcare emergency room at the time after all, and dare I say, never again not for me. For those in the medical field, my deepest respects, they truly are heroic beings in this world we live in. Anyway, the message that I wanted to convey here which I think is clear by now is that I slowly but surely discovered what it is I had to do to move toward the goal I had set in my life at the moment, which was graduation. In short, this translated to time management in my case, cutting all the fun stuff with friends, family as well as work and gym time that was getting in my way of my goals. Now this is not a recipe but rather an explanation of some of the sacrifices I had decided to make to reach my goals, but again everyone is different and this may translate to sacrificing a lot less or more than what I did depending on the individual.

Approaching graduation, I had a bigger goal to reach which was the whole purpose of me being in college in the first place, and the goal of course was to break into a career in tech which meant for me becoming a software engineer. After landing my first 2 internships my sophomore year of college, I started to realize that there was not a lot of work in the tech industry in my current hometown. Well I did not start to realize it, more I knew about it way beforehand as my original dream was to leave the city post graduation to work in a place like California which I knew to have been blooming with tech jobs since the 90s. What I meant to say is that chasing a career as a software engineer was most likely not going to be possible in my hometown, the town I grew up in was not only lacking in technology by a long shot but whatever jobs they had available were extremely scarce, volatile and offered below average pay. For some of the friends I met in college this was infuriating as they had decided to study something they were passionate about but were not willing to make the sacrifice of moving elsewhere to make a living of it. For me however this was a win-win and "my ticket" to paradise as I had said back in the day, I had no absolute problem moving elsewhere as I had not done much travel in my life at the time. Though I did understand the frustration when it came to the compensation some of the corporations were offering fresh graduates and yet still having an intense screening and interview process. Had I decided to have the same mindset as my colleagues of deciding to find a career in my hometown instead of being open to out of town options, I would have also been extremely frustrated and disappointed in the time spent going to college and such. I remember working at the hospital emergency room one time and attending to this patient, a lady and her son, who had come all the way from Austin, Texas. As I prepared to verify her medical insurance information I had told her to wait for me while I went to grab the paperwork and when I came back with actual paper she said to me "Oh my you actually meant paperwork, I thought you were just coming back with a tablet for me to sign stuff". I quickly laughed, and she added "this is crazy I have not had to sign any physical papers for a while now", I had then asked her if they just use a tablet for everything in Austin, Texas at the time this was 2016, she had said yeah that for that reason she was shocked. I have never lived in Austin, so I don't know if she was telling the truth or not, but regardless she was just reiterating the obvious to me, that my hometown was far behind in technology. In my brain, this translated to Austin, Texas becoming a potential candidate city for me to move to and start a software engineering career in, which seemed very exciting. There were multiple other instances like these that I won't go into detail here but fast-forward to graduation, I have landed my first full time role in the city of Indianapolis, Indiana and this was August 2018. I was dying of excitement to live in a new city, and experience new cultures, diversity and explore new opportunities within the tech industry, regardless of where that meant I'd end up. At this role I ended up being shipped frequently to the company's client locations which were mostly Dallas, Texas. It was this city within Texas that had first made me realize that a new tech hub within Texas was slowly emerging. I am not just referring to Dallas, but to cities like Houston, Austin and San Antonio where I witnessed companies like Deloitte, Chase, Intuit and many others from either side of the coast deciding to make the move or expand as opposed to staying in places like New York or California. Whether this was done as part of their business strategies or not was not of relevance to me, but rather a feel of excitement about the fact that such corporations were choosing Texas as their new tech hub as opposed to your typical California or Seattle locations. It was then at this very moment that I had decided to interview with local corporations within the Dallas location, which turned out to be a good move as I eventually landed a role in this city, prompting my move back to my home state in a metroplex big enough for my liking. Not only that but I was now closer to family at a distance where they were finally willing to visit me, and as it turned out I had discovered some of my college friends to have been in the area as well which was another win for me. I will say though, even if I had been in a situation where I did not wish to leave my family and hometown, I probably would still have left to a different city to kick-start my career and gain some experience before deciding to come back and try again in my hometown with the gained knowledge and experience. Or after having gained a couple of years of experience, would have probably looked for a remote role (as those are now a thing in 2022) to move back to my hometown had that been the objective. To me, it just made sense, and it was in my mind the equivalent of any aspiring actor or music artist having to move to a place in Hollywood or something of the sort, to have direct access into the industry that they wish to work in. Not making this move could have been a major deciding factor as to whether or not they broke into their respective field, I am not saying this is the only way, but in most cases I see this as the clearest path to break into a field. These are just my thoughts thought and to this day, no I still don't live in California as my goals and point of views have changed drastically in light of recent events, but I have no regrets of living and or working where I currently am, I did what I had too, and I think that turned out for the best. Moral of the story is, do your research, eliminate any and all distractions keeping you from your goals, and do what is necessary to start your career or meet your goals. Sometimes this means little sacrifices like cutting Friday nights out with friends to make room to study, or sometimes it means colossal tasks like moving to a completely new and distant city to jump start your career.

Getting Noticed

This kind of feels like a continuation of "doing what you must to break in" and in part it kind of is, so I will try to keep this brief. One of the most difficult things of breaking into tech for someone with no prior experience is of course getting their foot in the door. I think this applies to most if not all industries, but getting noticed is the first step to breaking into any industry and I had trouble understanding how to make noise without having any prior related experience. Well to me that just meant making my own experience or at least attempting to do so. And sometimes this is what is needed, to take one's matters into one's hands and make it happen. I had become so determined that I was willing to even intern for free in exchange for putting relevant experience in my resume to get my foot in the door. Luckily my internships ended up being paid but as stated earlier I was willing to do what it took and that ended up having to also take up freelance work. Though this freelance work ended up being almost free to my at the time client which was a former manager of mine from a non-related software gig I had in the past, it ended up being of great help to my resume. I say this because during my interview for my first full time software engineering role, this was one of the two projects interviewers had me show off and walk them through the functionalities of it that were implemented. So every little bit of experience and professional projects done count, especially when one is starting out in the industry.

I have not yet talked about how I landed that interview in the first place, though, and here is the scoop.

About a month or two prior to graduation, a classmate and friend of mine was talking to me about this company he was interviewing for, that had told him was willing to make an offer for a start date post graduation. He had just finished the third round of their interview process and was awaiting a response from them, the interviewees had asked him for any additional recommendations to be sent their way. Luckily, as he was just talking to me about his interview experience, I had asked him to recommend me if he had not already sent recommendations their way. Without hesitation, he decided to recommend me, and I was then contacted for an interview a month before graduation by the same company my friend had just interviewed. Having no plans yet after graduation, I decided to take the opportunity to also interview with this same company that my friend had just interviewed with, since I already had an idea of what was to come in the interview from just talking to him. Fast-forward to a couple of weeks from graduation, both my friend and I end up getting offers to work in Indianapolis, Indiana. My friend ends up denying the offer as this meant he'd have to move away from his family, I on the other hand had accepted and decided to move forward. Whether or not my candidacy would have been considered had I not had a referral from my friend remains a good question. I will however note that I do think this sped up the interview request process significantly as they specifically stated I had been referred by a very good candidate and that they were looking for more "top talent". This was not the only friend willing to refer me. I had others willing to give my reference to employers that had already made an offer to them and these were employers in industries like aerospace, arms defense, and automotive manufacturing among others. Though after landing this first offer letter, I quit looking and interviewing for other companies, denying many of the requests made by my peers to refer me to their employers, which is one thing I do regret. I had done so due to pride and intimidation, as I wanted to move to a place where I knew no one, and form new connections, something I did end up doing before moving back to Texas. This was the pride part of me taking over and I say intimidation because after finding out what the interview process looked like for me at these companies my friends wanted to refer me to, I became convinced that the interview was going to be a waste of time and humiliation for me. I say this because the interview processes as my friends had described it to me involved things like a one or two hour long presentation session to the employer of my experiences and skills within the software industry, where they spend the rest of the day asking me questions about it. Or some of these processes involved 5 day interview days with upper management and or higher ups as I like to call them. Whatever the case, both of these scenarios made me extremely uncomfortable as I consider myself to be an extreme introvert, so the idea that I had to entertain some people for 2 hours seemed impossible, much less doing so for 5 days, as I tend to come off as an extremely dull and quiet persona. If I ever considered myself good at entertaining a public onstage or via PowerPoint presentation, I don't think I would have considered aspiring to become a software engineer, those were my exact thoughts. And for such stupid reasons I had decided to deny requests from colleagues to refer me to their employers as a potential candidate, something one should not do as connections can be extremely beneficial to have. I no longer have most of these connections but notice how it was the use of my very first connection or "referral" that got me noticed at one of these engineering companies in the IT or Tech industry, that ended up being handy. As stated in the beginning, getting noticed in the industry can be difficult when starting up even if you have shown to have freelance work, internship experience or both. Attempting to stand out in any positive way is what tends to work in a candidate's favor, and if that means attaining a referral from a high profile employee or person, then by all means, I encourage doing whatever it takes to get noticed.

I would always set new goals after the old ones had become fulfilled. For example, once you have broken into the industry and have begun to work and gain experience as a software engineer, what is next, right? I would constantly ask myself this question, and it arose quickly, a year after having worked full time as a software engineer. I was never one to care much for titles, but I knew that the higher the title the higher the compensation, privileges and sometimes that meant more projects to choose from. So my goal had become to move up the rank from an associate engineer to a mid-tier engineer. After 2 years after working as an associate engineer, I had discovered that in order to move up the ranks, 2 criteria had to be met. One was that x number of years of experience had to be attained, and two was that the candidate had to have already been operating at the rank or tier level they wish to be promoted to in order to move to that level. My employer from 2019 would sporadically let me know that criteria number two was constantly met on my end, but due to restriction number one being total years of experience, they could not yet promote me from associate to mid-tier level. Eventually though, this first criteria was met, and I had been promoted to mid-tier level engineer, and it all seemed a great but a bit anti-climactic for me as the salary raise and compensation was higher but not to what I had expected or calculated it to be. The reason being, as explained by my employer at the time, was because the rest of the increase supposedly took effect six months after the candidate had worked as a mid-tier level engineer based on their performance. Meaning that if after six months the candidate is evaluated to still be performing at an associate level as opposed to the level of their newly promoted role, then no additional salary increase would be awarded, and on the contrary the increase was to be granted. However, as mentioned before, not only was I already performing at least mid-tier level as stated by my employer spontaneously but when the evaluation came I was approved to receive an additional salary increase that even after six additional months passed by, it never came. Luckily before deciding to speak to my employer about the promised salary increase that never came, six months after my promotion, I was confronted with a decision to make from another company I had interviewed with, three weeks before I had decided to speak up about the matter. I mean to say that just as I was about to get on the phone with my, at the time, current employer to ask about what happened to the promised salary increase that usually comes with a promotion. I instead ended up taking a call from another company that had decided to make me an offer I just could not pass up. This offer would not only grant me the title of mid-tier level software engineer that I had just been promoted to at my current workplace but would pay me far more than what my employer at the time could offer, even with the recent promotion I had earned, breaking my way into my first six figure role. So of course, the decision was a no-brainer, and I still ended up getting on the phone with my current employer, but not to complain about the salary increase that never came, and rather to give them my two weeks notice instead. They of course tried to retain me as I had only been six months at my newly acquired role, but when they asked to see what my offer salary was in an effort to counter it, they were unable to do so and I ended up making the move to my now employer of over 2 years as of 2020. I don't know if updating my resume as soon as I was granted the role of mid-tier software engineer had any influence on this company reaching out to me via linked in requesting me to interview for them or not. But as a rule of thumb I try to keep my resume up to date as much as possible whether I am looking for new opportunities or not, to stay in the radar of these recruiters as much as possible, should there ever be an emergency or need for it. Just one of many so-called "strategies" I have come up with to still "get noticed" by the industry out there that is ever-changing, as there will always be competition in this industry like many others.

Define Your Own Path

Not everyone will take the same route you have in reaching whatever goal they have set in mind. Everyone ends up breaking into the software industry in their own unique way, or at least that is what I came to know, and it is entertaining listening to each of my friends unique experience when I ask them about it. I witnessed friends receive six figure offers straight after graduation, but I also witnessed others like myself who only cared about breaking into the industry as a full time engineer. I have also witnessed friends that did not necessarily want to jump into the workspace quite yet and instead enjoyed pursuing further education and or research work as PhD candidates. As I have stated many times, everyone is different, and for that reason I encourage people to focus on themselves and no one else when it comes to fulfilling one's goals.

I will take the example of my friend, who not only was the first one to receive an offer letter among our group of friends, but also was one of the first to jump into a six-figure deal. This person was extremely talented, smart, disciplined and just straight up talented if I have not already mentioned that. He was one of those guys that was just about good at almost if not everything he tried, to me that was raw talent, but he also had a strong work ethic. That combination of dedication AND talent are two qualities very difficult to find in one single person, and he had these qualities. So believe me when I say that this was the type of person that unlike me had no trouble whatsoever juggling a full time job and being a full time student on top of also having extracurricular activities. A fun fact as well is that this guy rarely, and I mean this when I say this he rarely had to study for exams if at all, with the exception of the final exam and I know this because he would use me as a study partner since we had most classes together. I've only met two people like this in my life and this was one of them, his memory was so efficient and reliable that it heavily aided him on exams, which is why he would rarely need to study, as he had explained to me. He was able to replay every single lecture he had in his head along with every page of a textbook he ever read without any trouble remembering, as he'd put it. This to me was a gift, this screamed raw talent to my face but also made sense as to why school came so easy to him, that he had enough energy and effort to take on more tasks at once. In contrast to someone like me who had to take remedial math and reading courses his entire life even through college, and most days can barely remember what he had for breakfast. This guy was a prodigy in my eyes, and no, this is not me making excuses for my "failures" or the way I ended up doing things. I am simply describing the distinct personality types and their deltas to highlight the qualities of each person of interest within this story. Anyway, like most if not all of us who entered the workforce, my friend ended up using a connection he had to land an interview for a major aerospace company a month before graduation hit. Being a humble fresh graduate, my friend was not looking for a high salary but rather just looking to enter the software engineering industry as his main objective. So with that said, when he received an offer after a successful interview performance with this aerospace company, that offer ended up being a nice 6-figure salary promise for his role, post graduation. Now whether this was because of pure luck, or simply his raw talent and hard work that probably aided in his performance, I can't say for sure, but would not be surprised if it was indeed the latter. I on the other hand did not have such a generous offer, but also simply took the first offer that came my way without looking any further.

I had another friend within our group who was the complete opposite of this particular friend I just described, that ended up working for one of the major tech giants out there, and this giant is known as Microsoft. Not to say this friend of mine was not talented because he was in his own way of problem-solving, but from my and my other friend's observations, this guy did just barely enough to get through or pass a course. In other words, he wasn't your highly valued A student as my previous friend was but was instead a "just enough" student or as our professors loved to say at our university a "c" student. Now nothing wrong with being a c student at all in my opinion, if that is all you need to get a degree. I remember this saying that my generation invented that used to go something like "c's get degrees", that always made me laugh. Anyway to not get off-topic here but the only reason I am describing the type of student my friend was, is to show that even if you don't graduate with the best GPA possible, or you were someone like me who struggled through school to get by, there is still hope to work in whatever industry or company your heart desires. All it takes is patience, determination and perseverance, I got denied 4 times before finally getting a call from my current employer to interview with them. Back to the story though, I chose to speak about this particular friend as he was the second one in our group to have secured a six-figure deal with a tech giant like Microsoft. Now again, whether this was an influence of some connection he had inside or if he simply proved himself through all the interview rounds Microsoft put in front of him, It did not matter as he had simply found a way to make his dream a reality. He had made it in our eyes and though it was a bit shocking to us as we admitted to each other the minute we found out, we also recognized that there was nothing shocking about it, as his grades did not truly reflect the talent in problem-solving he displayed at times. In short, grades are not necessarily everything, as there may not be an accurate representation of one's real time skills when they are applied. On that note, I actually cannot remember a time I ever got asked about my GPA, which I guess is a good indicator of what employers actually look for. That is not to say one should just do the bare minimum at school, as I can also see how it could serve to one's best interest when looking for work. Regardless, in my opinion one should always do their best when attempting to reach a goal they have set their mind to, as the outcomes can be very good learning experiences. In the end everyone's path looks different and sometimes that path can be very un-predictable regardless of what is seen in "the book cover" of a human being. I simply hoped to inspire effort in trying one's best at reaching their goals set by sharing not just my own but my colleague's experiences at reaching their own goals, despite how distinct each of our personalities and paths ended up being. Our goal was one and the same "breaking into the software industry full time" but our paths and experiences to that end goal were all unique in their own way.

CAREER PATHS IN SOFTWARE ENGINEERING

The paths or as I like to call them "branches" of work one can take in software engineering are extremely broad in my opinion, and therefore will only cover the ones I am most familiar with. I have worked in some of these areas of work, which can feel like rather specialties of focus within the software industry. For example, when my career was kick-started, I worked specifically in mobile development for IOS mobile phones. For those not familiar with software mobile technology, IOS is simply short for iPhone Operating System. So, in short, my first software related work experience was in working with IOS mobile applications for the university I graduated from. Roughly around the same time, I had found an internship that allowed me to transition onto a different line of work within software, that being web development and enhancement of an existing application in the PHP programming language. Later having jumped into consulting, and though being trained as a full stack developer on my first consulting role, I ended up taking projects for clients related to chatbot application enhancement for their sites. Chatbot enhancement is exactly what it sounds like, a chatbot on someone's website or service that is used to start a chat conversation with the customer instead of having them wait to talk to human support waiting on a hot line or something. I guess this could still go under the web development branch of work, but will talk about it either way, since I have seen open positions for this specific feature under the name "chatbot developer". The last and latest branch of work I have dealt with that I feel comfortable sharing information about is a role that is a little more infrastructure related. In short as my title describes this line of work deals with not just the development side of things but the operations that is where the term "DevOps" comes from. Nowadays, racks of physical servers sitting in a warehouse are becoming more and more a thing of the past. Server space and "availability" zones are now services a corporation can buy and or subscribe to, without having to invest in actual warehouses themselves to store racks of servers in. These server spaces can be rather reserved and used via software as a service subscription or something close to this where everything is managed via a single application or website like "Amazon

Web Services". Also, when I say infrastructure I don't just mean the setup of servers for applications to run on, but things like networking traffic management, active directories and all the systems required for any application to be live and running. Though I did not directly work in the actual setup of infrastructure, I was still trained to learn to use certain platforms for automating software deployment and scaling software applications, such as Kubernetes and pivotal cloud foundry. Additionally, a big part of my role in troubleshooting such platforms was performance testing on an internal platform a team of mine made to see what architectural changes the platform needed if any to handle heavy load traffic and scaling as needed during high peak traffic times. What I mean to say is that software testing can be a whole career of its own, and will therefore also go a bit into detail as to what it was like doing nothing but testing a software product for a corporation. Sounds crazy, I know, but there was a staggeringly impressive process to just setting up the test material or scripts for running on a software. Now these are just branches within software itself that I have worked in and will expand upon, by no means is this a limited list of all paths an engineer could take. There are plenty of other roles out there to choose from such as cybersecurity, systems architect, Artificial intelligence engineer, IT project manager, video game developer, data scientist, computer programmer just to name a few. Also, some of these are not just branches specific to software engineering itself, but to the umbrella above being "computer science" in general. I only bring this up as most universities I have seen tend to guide their students to acquire a degree in computer science if they wish to work in the IT, software, or other related engineering field. I will briefly talk about this and what one can potentially do when one aspires to transition into a different engineering field within the computer science umbrella. I am referring to scenarios where a person's experience in engineering has been entirely in web development for example, but this person wishes to transition onto a system's engineering position or a cybersecurity position which they may have never worked in, in their career as a web developer. Though these are both fields falling within the computer science umbrella the transition may still be a bit of a hiccup and the person has no prior experience in the field they wish to transition to and of course there are always exceptions. There are also tiers of positions one can and should take into considerations when becoming an engineer. Companies usually like to start their less experienced employees as associates, eventually moving up to just "software engineer" to later transition into a senior and perhaps a manager role or further if they wish to go further. I will also cover this tier system that corporations like to follow, briefly, and talk about what a promotion was for me and what lies ahead of me and many other engineers in my position. Anyway, read on if you're interested to know what the work is like in each respected area listed below and or wish to use the information found to compare with other roles of interest.

Mobile App Development

It is no secret that the way a smart mobile device is used is through the help of small software components called applications or "apps" as the modern person would say. Every action the phone is prompted to take is done through the use of an application. If the user wants to send a text to someone, the messages app is used on an iPhone app by default to send a message, otherwise it is the messages app by google for android. Performing a call or literally any other action is the same when done in a phone, it is done through an application that the phone either already carries by default or has been downloaded. So with that said, it is no wonder that positions like android developer, mobile developer and iPhone developer tend to exist. Notice the word android and iPhone on some of the listed positions, and these are exactly what they sound like. Meaning, if you wish to work on applications that are solely and explicitly made for android operating systems or android based phones, you can do so by looking for positions that read "android" mobile developer. Vice versa, if you wish to work for solely apple based applications made for iPhone explicitly, one would look for openings in "IOS" mobile development. Also note that just because a developer might have experience in working on one mobile operating system like android it does not mean that if they wish to work in a role that requires them to touch both android and apple operating systems, that they may not be considered it may actually turn out to be quite the contrary. Not always the case, but as technology has evolved, this is becoming more and more the case thanks to the evolving technology available today. Platforms have emerged that now allow the engineer to code an entire application in one technology, as opposed to two or more separate ones per operating system to deploy to. For example, instead of writing one codebase version of an application for android based phones and also writing an entire different codebase for iPhone based users, the developer can now write one single codebase that can be deployed to both apple and android users simultaneously. For this reason, through the use of today's technologies and programming languages if a candidate only has experience in developing android phone based apps but not apple based apps this candidate can and will still be considered for a "mobile position" for android and iPhone based applications, as the knowledge they possess tends to be enough to write a single codebase. This single codebase can then be translated into whatever additional device they want to deploy the application to, be it iPhones or something else. This also depends on how corporations like to handle the development and deploy-ment of their applications to both the Apple Store and google store. There are times where corporations still prefer 2 separate codebases, one for iPhones and the other for android phones, for a variety of reasons. These reasons can be things like performance requirements that perhaps are not met as intended if dealing with a single codebase that was translated onto each respective phone type to deploy to. It can also be that the capabilities of the tools they have used are still very primitive and therefore not all the code written can be translated properly, which may end up meaning more work than if they had gone the traditional route. Regardless of the reason, it is important to note that corporations may still want to go through the traditional route of constructing mobile applications for both android and iPhones, as opposed to having a single codebase that is translated onto these respected devices.

Through my experience, there are certain things one needs to take into account when developing applications for either android or iPhone. One of the major components we had to take into account when designing a mobile app for the university I graduated from back then, during my internship, were the guidelines the Apple Store put in place for us. Though these were usually housekeeping tasks like icon dimensions for different versions of the iPhone, we also had to deal with letting the user know how their data was to be used. This meant that we, the developers, had to provide a link in the app store submission process that is to take the user to a series of pages for them to read from and find out how their information is to be used, aka "privacy policy". And yes, I am talking about the part where after a user downloads an app, they are prompted to either accept or decline the privacy policy and terms and conditions presented to them. This was definitely something I did not think I had to deal with as a developer, but it turned out we did, so it caught me by surprise and just wanted to note that. At the end of the day, how complex these are truly depends on what the app does and how complicated it is. I have heard that submitting an application to the Google store for android phone users is not as strict, and therefore developers can push out significantly more applications through android than through the Apple Store. I have not actually confirmed this to be true or not, but I would not be surprised if it is, and I encourage anyone that is curious to do their own research. Regardless, whether developing for IOS or just android based phones there will always be guidelines a developer will have to follow to make it through the respective store they are submitting to, be it the apple or the Google store for android. Another thing to note is that when submitting an application for an app to be on the Apple Store as I noticed on my internship, the developer will first be required to purchase an annual membership of 99 dollars a year to be able to have their application on the app store once all approvals are granted. Not only that, but if the developer charges for a service via the app they have placed on the app store, Apple likely will take a percentage of those sales made through the application of the developer. Again, this is information that I remember seeing back in 2018, so I'd advise anyone reading this to fact-check these statements, but It would not surprise me if these fees still exist. Anyway, working as an iPhone app developer or "IOS developer" was a very pleasant experience, and for reasons stated earlier I would also get calls from recruiters to take on roles that were either purely android phone based or both for iPhone and android development. Therefore, I encourage anyone with any mobile development experience to take on any mobile related opportunity they wish to try out even if they feel they don't have the skill set to do so as there may still be similarities between prior experiences.

Web Development

Websites to this day are still widely used worldwide and do not seem to be going anywhere in the near future, even with the transition onto web 3. Regardless, working on websites for a living can be really exciting and rewarding in terms of career development. There is a big market for freelance work when it comes to web development, though I don't have much experience in this domain, I have known people that do end up making a living off of freelance work alone. This can sound very seducing, as you'd be working on your own terms, so to speak, once settled in financially. Like most things in life though, there are always trade-offs, for example as a freelance developer you'd have to look for your own health and life insurance as well as manage your own retirement funds on your own versus when working under a corporation. A major perk though could be how much one decides to charge for their services, assuming reasonable quality work is offered of course, but this is what I mean by working on your own terms and some-what achieving "financial freedom". Now that is to say we assume absolute best case scenario when performing free-lance web development services, it isn't something that is done overnight or with the first couple of clients. As I always say of course though, take this with a grain of salt, the one time I did do some freelance web dev work for one of my former work managers I ended up charging little to no money. My reason for this was simple, I was attempting to break into the software industry at the time and saw more value if the experience was engraved on my resume as opposed to charging a little more money for what was a short-lived project. My focus was on the marathon, not the sprint, as my end goal was to end up working in software for a corporation at the time. Everyone's goals are different, though, and my only purpose talking about these options is to let the reader know what career paths one can take when it comes to work in the web development domain.

Speaking of web development options, these types of positions are usually split into one of three categories. The backend developer, front end or full stack developer, I have not yet been fortunate enough to work professionally as a front end or full stack developer, but my entire career has been focused on the "backend" side of things, so most of my insight will focus on that area. The backend usually refers to the work that is to be done "behind the curtain" meaning all the work related to functionality alone, this is the piece that makes a button work on a website when it is clicked. Otherwise, nothing would occur if such a button is clicked without any sort of backend functionality wired to it. The front end as you can probably guess refers to the opposite, meaning what the software interface looks like, this is the part that brings to life the way a website looks with all its buttons, menus, tabs and all. Full stack development is the whole burger in one piece, that is to say the front end wired along with its respected backend.

Also, if needed, additional database functionality is added to display data on a frontend for when a website is loaded or a button is prompted to display data of some sort. This piece usually talks to the backend or is part of the backend, it can be designed in many ways but is part of the whole "full stack" of technologies used for web development. As I stated earlier my entire career I have been doing back-end work, even though I received training as a full stack developer back in 2018 I have yet to put all of it to use. When it comes to web development, corporations use the words "back end", "front end" and "full stack" exclusively for web based roles when they need to specify what type of work they are hiring for. Do note however that these words are not exclusive to just web development and may be used for any type of application, for example a corporation may just need a candidate that can work on a back-end for an already developed mobile application that has a front end ready or vice versa. These words are often used interchangeably when it comes to software, but are definitely more common when it comes to web development specifically. From experience, I can confirm this, as my title on paper has never been backend, front end or full stack developer. I do notice corporations like to keep the title as broad as possible, as I usually also do work that does not fall under any of the three criteria just mentioned.

One other thing I do want to talk about, as you may or may not be thinking about this like I once was, is the subject of pay when it comes to web development. As I mentioned earlier, full stack development means the entire burger as a whole, meaning dealing with back end, front end, and other layers that may be needed in between. Naturally since one is not only dealing with one piece of web dev, like the front or backend but the whole technology stack as a whole then this might mean that pay may be higher for a full stack developer as opposed to a role fully focused on backend or front end alone, right? Well it depends but in short, my answer would be no, not exactly. This can sometimes be the case if you're for example maybe working for a startup, but from experience I generally find this not to be the case. For what reason, I still don't know but have come to the conclusion that this is because these roles are designed for the individual to focus in one particular area, be it backend for example, across not one but as many projects as needed. I can only assume it is the same for full stack developers, and this information I have gathered from talking to my peers in the industry and comparing what they discovered with what I have encountered, the conclusions seem to be consistent. Again, these are just conclusions and my colleagues and I best guess as to why the pay for a full stack role is rarely if ever higher than a role for a front end or web developer. They are usually somewhat on par with each other, unless the project is temporary and for a single one time project, but that concept tends to apply to anything not just web development.

Software Consulting

My first official full time role as a software engineer was in software consulting services, this company offered services of any kind related to software for their clients. Literally anything be it web development, data visualization, machine learning, mobile development, database administration, development operations work, I.T. work you name it. Once onboarded with this employer, they offered a 4-month training to all new hires in different areas depending on their expertise. I was hired to offer consulting services to their clients in the form of web development, which meant that I was to attend the full stack development training for the duration of the 4 months prior to actually begin working with clients. Long story short, after the 4-month training is successfully completed through the passing of a technical assessment exam, the employee then becomes eligible to begin working with clients. As such I expected to be mapped to projects that needed any form of full stack development but since none were currently available at the moment and the only thing that had come up was a project in chatbot enhancement. My manager at the time then decided to map me to such a project after 2 additional weeks of training in chatbot development. In case you are wondering what chatbot development is, well it is exactly what it sounds like. Have you ever seen those annoying robots on webpages pop up as soon as the page loads up, when you navigate to literally just about any website on the internet these days? Yes, that little robot asking you how it can help you, to avoid contacting the actual human support team, that is the chatbot I am talking about. Anyway, since there were only projects available for chatbot enhancement on client's products, I took the projects to avoid being idle until something of interest popped up. As for the tech stack, the chatbot my team enhanced for our client at the time was composed of "google dialog flow" technology, and was integrated with the client's backend which was a "java based technology called spring". Feel free to perform a quick google search on the quoted items if these terms sound like a foreign language to you. The technology stack used here is not of much importance, so I won't go into detail on it, but I did want to provide a sneak peek on the potential tech stack used for when dealing with chatbots. Anyway, this project at the time was a project that was calculated to last a year given the amount of work required to be done for the client. This was back in 2018, in pre-pandemic times, so my team and I were required to work out of the client's location for the duration of the project, which at the time was Dallas, Texas. We were allowed to stay and work from our employer's office at the Indianapolis location for 2 weeks out of the month, and got reimbursed for all the expenses we had each month where we worked in the Dallas location. Once this project is finished, the employee is typically mapped onto new projects as their manager's see fit or as needed by clients of theirs. So after this project with the Dallas client was over, I got immediately mapped to a project based out of Seattle, Washington but ended up, moving onto a better role relocating to Dallas that following year.

In summary, if you like travel and perhaps swapping around different technologies of interest within your career, perhaps software consulting companies may be within your best interest to try out. Some well known honorable mentions of such companies are the following but not limited to Cognizant, Accenture, Wipro and HCL Technologies. Do note that ever since the pandemic though, instead of consultants being required to travel and work from the client's headquarters offices, it is now more common that they stay working remotely from home. The consultants I have worked with at my current role, have been remote since 2020, and I have yet to know what they look like. Even the consultants who have left my current team that I talked to say that they are still working remotely after being mapped to a different client in an entirely different city. I can't confirm that every single consulting firm is having their employees work remotely since 2020, but my friends at some of these firms have been working fully remotely since 2020. So my mistake there is a slight correction, if instead of travel you prefer the "work from home" lifestyle in 2022 and potentially 2023, then consider looking for roles that specialize in software consulting services for clients. Not all consulting firms work the same, but I wanted to provide my experience as a basis or template as to how they operate, and that way help you the reader decide if this is a route of interest when it comes to working in software. There are some things other firms do better than the one I worked with, like paying for work related expenses upfront instead or via reimbursement, like my previous employer did for me. Or giving you time to prepare to ship out to a particular client's headquarters office versus having you shipped overnight onto the client's location. In summary, the way these consulting firms like to operate is in the following way. Once the employee is onboarded, they will receive official training in the technical area in which they have most experience in or show to be somewhat proficient in. After successful training, they are allocated to a project, meaning mapped to a contract with a client who is in need of their skill set or service. If the candidate does not currently possess the skills needed to perform the work for the client they are mapped to, the candidate will receive additional training to acquire said skill set. Once that is completed, the employee is shipped out to the client's location, though as of 2022 the employee instead works remotely for the duration of the project. This cycle then repeats itself when the employee is mapped to a different client once the contract with their previous client is complete. The employee can also choose to reject a project they have been mapped to or leave an existing project up to a number of times before they receive a strike on their profile. In my case I could reject projects up to 3 times per year, but I assume this number probably varies between companies, some may not even have such a limitation or may actually have a worse number. Sometimes these contracts can be negotiated with the client through the employee's own manager. I'm talking about negotiating things like days of stay at the client's location or duration of the contract and things like that. As I mentioned though these things need to be brought to the employee's manager first before letting the client know and usually the manager would let the employee know if they are able to negotiate such things or not. Additionally, these "contracts" between the client and the consulting firm are not to be misunderstood to be contract to hire agreements that hiring companies tend to set up with their clients. When working in a consulting firm, the employee is employed by the consulting firm and therefore is ineligible to get hired by the client directly unless the employee chooses to leave the role immediately, but there are usually restrictions set in place for such scenarios. When I say contracts in terms of being an employee of a consulting firm, I mean a working agreement of the work to be performed for a particular client as a consultant for said client or customer. Well like anything else in life these are the pros and cons of working for a software consultant firm from my perspective. I did not go into depth about the clients because the clients can be literally any corporation that needs a specific service, my firm worked with clients like Verizon, Boeing, Pepsi, American Airlines among many others. Nevertheless, software consulting can be fun and a great way to get exposure into different areas of software and figure out from there what technology an individual enjoys working with the most.

Software Testing

One of my college professors once said that the role of software tester was one of the most underrated jobs out there that a software engineer could work in. I genuinely did not know at the time if he was joking or not, but I actually didn't care much because the word "tester" just did not seem appealing to me at all. That said, I thought I'd probably never end up working for such a role throughout my career, but that turned out to be an incorrect conclusion to make. One of the very first things I was assigned to do with my latest employer was performance testing, or addressing non-functional requirements to be politically and technically correct. Before I go into what the day-to-day job was like and its pros and cons, I will talk a little about these so-called non-functional vs functional requirements. Starting off with the "functional" requirements, when it comes to software, these types of requirements are usually requirements that focus on what the software being built is supposed to do. So when a software engineer begins to work on the software project assigned, there usually exists a set of requirements that must be met before the developer can call their work done. In the event of these requirements being functional requirements as stated earlier, then the type of work being done on said software would focus on the software's features or more like functions. The emphasis is on what the software is supposed to do, as stated earlier. So for example, if I am building a mobile app that is supposed to be able to track a user's location as they move regardless of whether or not they are in a fast moving vehicle, then that requirement is part of the functional requirements needed to be fulfilled to complete such software. The "functionality" of this mobile app is "tracking the user's location at all times", this is what the mobile app does or what its desired functionality is, hence an example of what a functional requirement can be. The non-functional requirements are not as intuitive and tend to focus more on the quality properties of a software that are of relevance. For example, these "qualities" can be things like "availability" where a system is "available" meaning fully operable and ready to perform its functions when the user needs it to do so. That may mean a system being available at least between hours of 9am to 5pm on any given day or perhaps 12 hours a day 4 days a week if it is a more crucial piece of software for example. Another example of a non-functional requirement is "resiliency", and this translates to the software of interest being able to provide an acceptable form of service, even after faults or errors have been encountered with the use of such a software system. This is what a resilient software is described to be, a software that even when faults have affected it, has the power to still deliver to its customers the functionalities at hand that it offers to a certain degree. The last example I want to draw attention to is the quality of "scalability". This non-functional quality attribute is one that focuses on the performance of the software of interest and how it is affected when demands for such software's resources increase or decrease. Does performance go down when heavy loads of traffic are hitting the system? Is there a big lag difference? Or does its performance remain unaffected? If so, for how long? How long until the system breaks and its availability becomes non-existent? These are some of many questions asked when addressing non-functional requirements related to the software products being built by the developer. Note that I only listed about three non-functional requirements off the top of my head, but there are many more out there that can be found or encountered when gathering requirements for constructing software. Some of these requirements would not be listed to the developer explicitly as they are "implied" due to the criticality of said systems. For example, if a developer is programming a very crucial piece of software like a flight management system, a system that is meant to fly an aircraft without an active intervention from a pilot. Then not only is this piece of critical software implied to be required to be able to perform its functionality with extreme precision, but such a software will need to have reliable performance, and availability qualities to avoid critical malfunction, as there are lives at stake with such a system so to speak.

As stated previously though I did not think I would even work in software testing specifically as a job role, I did end up acquiring such experience and will now go into detail as to what that was like for me. The reason I brought up non-functional and functional requirements is because as a software tester, one is usually in charge of addressing either one of these requirements or both. The whole point of testing at the end of the day is not just to make sure a specific requirement was completed, but to make sure the built system is made to the expected quality for the customer's needs with as minimal bugs in it as possible. Generally as a software engineer one is taught to test everything they have built themselves or when performing error-prone tasks such as integration or maintenance, this is the general type of testing that is just due diligence, so I won't go so much into depth about this. I will focus more on the roles in the context of software, whose main purpose or task is to focus on the testing side of software, be it for functional or non-functional requirements. These types of roles usually have titles like "Software Tester", "QA Tester", "Performance Tester" or something of the sort in their job description. Anyway, a day in the life of a tester, specifically one focused on addressing non-functional requirements, goes somewhat like the following. First the on-functional requirements to be addressed are defined for such tester and these can be more than one, in fact it is rarely ever just one, but that is also a possibility I suppose.

Once that goal is set in place of reaching scalability and availability of 10 hours per day at minimum, for example, the tester begins to get things ready for when testing is done. This usually means picking the tool to perform testing with if there is not one specified to use or no enterprise level tool available yet. Now, depending on what tool is picked out for testing, the tester may or may not need to perform additional setup for when testing begins. Some Testing tools generate metric reports on their own on the values of the software tested, but not all do. That said, there usually needs to be some sort of metric monitoring system in place to read the vitals of the software system for when it is tested. I am referring to things like CPU usage, incoming HTP requests if applicable, current incoming traffic, ram usage and things of that nature within the system to be tested, note that this is a super limited list of properties to look at. These listed components will fluctuate up and down when a system is stress tested, for example, and therefore it is important to have a monitoring system in place for when the software testing is done. The term stress testing here is used in reference to testing a software system by injecting heavy loads of traffic to it until failure of the software's function is achieved. Once testing is done and all the desired information is gathered from the metric monitoring system set in place, the tester can analyze its data to decide what further testing is needed if any or what architectural changes the software needs from the development side to fulfill the specified non-functional requirements. If it is decided that architectural changes need to be made to enhance the software's performance, or in other words: fulfill the non-functional attribute specified. Then, once those enhancements are complete, software testing resumes on the system again to gather new metrics that are hopefully a major improvement of what was seen in the prior testing trial. If even after tweaks, the software still does not meet the desired non-functional requirements defined by the customer or stakeholder. The system is further tweaked and tested until its performance reaches the desired quality presented in the non-functional requirements definition. The software is of course tweaked each time according to the decisions derived from the analysis of its metric data fluctuations experienced during the testing trials, and these decisions are made as a team, rarely ever by a single person. In other words, the data gathered from each test trial, becomes useful insightful information that helps determine changes needed to be made to the software being tested, to fulfill its specified non-functional requirements. Once requirements are fulfilled, one could say that the job of the software tester is "completed". One very important thing to note though when dealing with non-functional requirements is that there will always be sacrifice when making quality decisions of a system. Here is an example to explain what I mean, if a software system is improved to have high scalability and resilience, while it may deliver on those qualities, it may also be sacrificing the system's performance and or response time. This would likely be due to the system focusing more on traffic handling and recovery from faults, which can both be main factors or lag or extended response times affecting the system's performance in the end. Most companies understand this at this point, and for that reason always list the non-functional requirement that they want the most emphasis on. In short, no matter what qualities a software system is improved to have, it will always be sacrificing in other areas, this is a problem that exists even in today's world of 2022. My experience as a software tester was very rewarding, but the only thing I did kind of notice as a con was, that in terms of programming or coding not much was done aside from creating the actual test scripts to use for testing. Aside from that, dealing with non-functional requirements as a software tester can be a great first step to learning about software architecture, and its behavior when it comes to certain architecture decisions.

The Tier Level System

So I have covered different engineering routes one can potentially branch into, but I have not talked about moving up in tech. I will be honest, moving up the corporate ladder was never my end goal or dream, but if that is your end goal, hopefully my experience can provide some insight as to what that route may look like. Now, at the time of writing this book I have only moved up the ladder a couple of times, and the first time was unintentionally. One thing I have learned over the years is how much companies value candidates with experience, the more, the better, or at least that is what it seems. I remember A co-worker telling me one time something along the lines of the corporate world being a longevity game. I don't remember the exact words, but he told me something like "once you're in you're in man, promotions and title changes come down to a matter of time within a company". Furthermore, I found this to be somewhat true, though of course, like almost anything in life there are exceptions such as layoffs, going out of business etcetera. Speaking from my own experience, once you've landed the role, it is relatively difficult for a company to decide to get rid of a new employee. This varies by company of course and their goals, don't get me wrong any corporation and I genuinely mean any, will not hesitate to get rid of an employee if it is in their best interest. But putting aside things out of one's control like budgeting costs that lead to layoffs and things of that nature, the employee would have to really be trying hard to get onto their employer's black list and end up demoted or let go. I'm talking about doing things like extreme downgrading in performance, eating company time away, or not completing any of the assigned work in time. This type of behavior will lead to poor performance reviews, which translate to disciplinary action or being let go of employment. Other than that, though, back to what my co-worker was trying to say by stating that the corporate game is a game of longevity. I believe what he meant to say is that as long as one does their due diligence within their role, the promotions will come when certain amounts of years of experience in the industry are reached. This does not mean the person cannot move up prior to attaining the required years of experience necessary to make it onto the next promotion. There are exceptions to this, if the employee can demonstrate to their employer that they are already operating at the level of the higher role, then this is a good flag for the employer to approve this person for a promotion. From experience though, and I think this applies to most companies, you as the employer have to speak up to leadership or your higher ups if this is the case, to get your work noticed. No one, and I mean no one, not a single soul within the company is on the lookout for someone who performs at a level higher than what they were hired for. I can't say this for every corporation in this world, but as far as I know this is not the case. Additionally, there may be times when an employee's performance is indeed noticed, but all you get is an electronic recognition certificate for your work and nothing more. This is why I encourage people to always speak up and not let the impostor syndrome take over, or feed you guilt-trips about being an entitled millennial or gen-z employee. If you as the employee feel your performance far exceeds that of your current role, then it is your responsibility to discuss this with your manager or leadership about a potential promotion opportunity if that is what you desire. Again, I can't speak for every company but from experience even when this work ethic and performance is acknowledged, the word "promotion" rarely comes into play. Be it because the employer really wants to play by the rules and wait until x number of years experience are reached, or because they don't have time etcetera, bottom line it doesn't hurt to try and ask about these promotion opportunities. The worse that can happen is that they say no, if any outcome more severe than a no occurs, then I'd question my position with the current employer. That said, there could be instances where even though one's performance is at a level higher than the role they possess, they may still be denied promotion opportunities. If this is the case, and you were really hoping for a promotion, or you need one, then maybe consider a shift within an internal team if possible, or an employer that values its employees on their skill set and performance as opposed to years in the industry. These companies can be somewhat hard to find or scarce, from what I've experienced, but they are out there. Now for those passive employees like myself who enjoy a peaceful career within their current role and don't really dream of moving up in corporate, I have some news. Eventually you may be unexpectedly, or as expected, promoted within your company, be it because you have reached a certain number of years in the industry, because your performance has been superb or both. However, if it was unexpected than more than likely this means you have reached x number of years of experience, at your current role which raised flags within the company you work for. This can be good, or I guess "bad" depending on what the person's goals are, always keep in mind that higher compensation usually comes with higher expectations. This may scream "disruption of work-life balance" within some folks, and hence the reason they may view an unanticipated promotion as a "bad" thing. Additionally, the "higher" pay that comes with the promotion may not be worth the extra ten or fifteen hours of overtime to employees, and that is completely understandable, at least from my point of view. But sometimes it turns out that it is, for example if you just made a big jump from let's say a senior engineer to manager or let's go bigger you go from manager to director, then that is a huge shift. Without a doubt you will inevitably be more busy than if you were in your manager role, but from what I've heard there is also a huge compensation package to make up for all the hassle. Notice that I am talking about big shifts here from an engineering role to a more leadership role, also notice that I said "from what I've heard" from friends as I am far from even becoming a manager at this point, so I can't say much from experience on those big promotions. Still, even so, there are folks out there that are not willing to spend time away from their family, growing kids, and loved ones like myself. These folks may view moments with loved one's as priceless and would rather stay in the position that keeps them happy, even if it means passing on a promotion. Just something to keep in mind when taking into consideration promotion's being offered at hand, these types of positions may be better for those who are willing to put in the sacrifices, or have not yet decided to settle down with a family. Either way, there is no wrong decision here, I am just noting things I've thought about when I experienced my first promotion, as it is easy to get hung up on the new compensation that comes with the promotion that we forget to think about the new responsibilities that also come with the position.

Like I mentioned before, if you as the employee find yourself perfectly happy within your current role, here are a couple of things you can do to pass up on the golden opportunity of the promotion presenting itself to you. One thing you can do is to look for employment elsewhere, with the same position or title you wish to keep. Look for employers that are willing to take you as a candidate for the position you are interested in, regardless of whether or not you have more years of experience than required for the position. If due to the experience you have, the companies would rather have you try out for a position you are trying to avoid in the first place, then consider maybe starting over by trying a more associate role in a different branch of engineering. Say for example you have 5 years experience in mobile android development in the java programming language, and you were about to be promoted to senior engineer but want to stay as a normal software engineer. Then consider interviewing in a different branch of work, like maybe working as a video game developer in the c++ programming language. Since you have no experience in the c++ language, you might want to consider applying for an associate role instead and working your way up there if desired. Another option is to switch teams within your own company to a management level that is okay with keeping you where you're at, without any promotions. Lastly, and the more justifiable solution is to talk to your manager about how you feel and why you prefer to stay at your current role, be professional of course but honest about why you want to stay in the same role. Again, the worst that could happen is you getting a promotion, otherwise you stay where you're at, do note though that this may only be temporary. In other words, you may just be delaying the inevitable, as eventually your pay raise will bleed into the range of the position you're the promotion offer is based on. For those that don't know, when working in not just the software industry but any white collar job, maybe even blue collar job or career the employee usually receives a raise of some sort every year that they remain loyal to their employer. Before you get excited, though, these are usually not big raises and tend to be based on 2 things, company performance and the employee's performance. But even if the employer's performance was not at its best by the end of year review, the employer still receives that performance bonus, just at a lower rate than usual, so it would be something like a 2 percent raise instead of 4, for example. Same with the company bonus, depending on company revenue, performance etcetera, the employer will receive a bonus of some sort, and sometimes no bonus if the company's numbers did not profit. Like anything else in life, though, nothing is guaranteed, and every company operates differently. From what I've seen and experienced, though, salary increases usually come, even when the employee's performance is not at the standard set by the company. This is what I mean by eventually bleeding into the salary range of the next tier level position, forcing the employer to promote their employee of interest.

With that said, I have learned the hard way that just because someone's title reads a tier higher than mine, that does not necessarily translate to this person having the skills required to operate at the position being displayed. Experiences like this get me thinking more and more by the day about what my colleague had told me of the workforce being a longevity game. This seems scary, but it is a total possibility that an individual may be promoted without first acquiring the skills needed to operate at the following tier. I have also witnessed engineers with heavy technical background and no people skills being promoted into leadership roles like a manager or director of some sort. This is probably due to the yearly salary raise explanation I gave earlier, since most engineering roles are capped at the "principal engineer" level, the only way to move up from there for an engineer is to move to a management role. The tier system is usually labeled as follows: the associate engineer, that is the beginner level, then you move over to software engineer or a mid-tier position, and after that come the senior engineers and later the principal or technical lead engineer which starts to consist of more meetings and less programming, this is a more leadership focused engineering role. Nonetheless, the point is that the highest position available for an engineer is the title of "principal engineer" as far as I can tell. Different companies will tweak the names of these positions to their liking, but the tiers of interest are usually consistent throughout most corporations, from what I've seen. Past the principal engineer role, you start to see more leadership types of roles like manager, senior software manager, associate director, director, then vice president etcetera. So don't get me wrong I'm all for promotions but this type of system of breaking into a managerial role with no prior people skills or managerial experiences, is in my opinion a setup for a chaotic team dynamic. Talking from my personal experience with "newly formed" teams and managers, this is how micromanagers and toxic workplaces are born. I am delighted that companies grant the opportunities for technical engineers to transition into managerial roles, but I am also against it, if there is no prior training provided for these engineers as to what their role is and how to approach its responsibilities. At any rate, nothing is easy in life but if you are an aspiring software engineer hoping to one day end up as a software manager or higher, then I guess good news this is totally a possibility without any prior management experience.

A final thing to note is that titles could potentially mean nothing in terms of what they offer as far as compensation and what the role consists of. For example, the Associate engineer working at YouTube could be making the equivalent of what a senior engineer makes at a consulting company. Meaning to say that although the associate software engineer is at the beginner level, two tiers below the senior, this engineer may be getting the same pay or more than its senior counterpart. I have seen this happen and have a few explanations as to why this could be the case but it essentially comes down to many factors. One such factor could be location, maybe the associate engineer works on site in the California Bay area, office and hence the salary being much higher to account for the cost of living. Compared to its senior engineer that lives in the state of Ohio where they may be getting their money's worth of real estate square footage. Another explanation for this could be company size and or budget, the associate is working for a well established company that is not only willing but able to offer its employees a very generous pay. The senior engineer may be with a company of mid to small size whose budget is really tight and therefore salaries may be affected throughout the whole enterprise. This company may be a startup in its very early stages and funding has yet to come perhaps. A third reason could be task differences in each respected role, perhaps the associate has a more intensive algorithmic problem solving role than that of the senior working at a company that is not technology based to begin with. Or perhaps the associate was simply a talented negotiator, you never know. These are just a few of the many factors that could have influenced compensation benefits within engineering roles, in different companies but bottom line titles are sometimes just that, titles on a paper they could mean nothing.

REMOTE WORK & THE EFFECTS OF THE 2019 PANDEMIC

It is 2022 as of the writing of this book, and to this day as far as I can tell the world is still having this battle with the covid-19 virus of 2019. I would go as far as to say that a new norm has rather emerged and we humans are simply learning how to co exist with this pandemic as opposed to trying to end it. Like many industries that were affected by the lockdown restrictions put in place, the software industry was of course no exception. At the time in 2019, I was working as a contractor in the software industry and knew that the lockdown would affect my role in one of the following ways. This lockdown either meant that my employer was going to close shop and close down all its offices or was going to find a way to work around the new lockdown restrictions set in place. Fortunately the latter took effect, but since our work was always done on our desktops at the corporate offices that were setup by the company's IT department, this turned out to be an additional expense for the company. This is due to the company having to purchase laptops for their employees to set up and take home to be able to work at home while the lockdown restrictions occurred. This was my first experience ever working remotely as a software engineer and though I was scared at the time of my future in the industry, I was also excited to be able to work from the comfort of my home. Not everything is always bunnies and flowers though, and though I am pro choice remote work I will also cover things that could be viewed as disadvantages. In short I think this pandemic simply sped up a lot of inevitable trends but also created opportunities and a drive for innovation around the world and its businesses. As I previously mentioned though this pandemic started in 2019, and there no longer are any lockdowns set in place, it still does not feel to be over as nothing ever went "back to normal". Instead I think humanity decided to stop trying and stabilize the virus that started the pandemic and has taken a more realistic approach of setting rules and protocols in place for coexisting with such a phenomenon. This is not as terrible as it sounds when it comes to the workplace though and you'll see what I mean in the preceding sections.

The Good and The Ugly

So, it is no secret by now that one of the things the 2019 pandemic brought to the software industry at the global level was remote work. Being able to work from the comfort of your home or, as 2022 would put it, "from wherever you please". Don't get me wrong, I know that there were jobs out there prior to the pandemic that already offered remote work opportunities. However, as far as I could tell these were very scarce and unknown to the average applicant, or at least for me and all the people I worked with this was the case. I don't know if I would have had to move away from my hometown if there were as many remote jobs available as there are today prior to the 2019 pandemic. Regardless, I remember the dream software job prior to the rise of remote work was to actually work in one of those crazy luxury corporate offices that were full of endless amenities. Yeah, I am talking about those google or apple like office settings where you get free food all day, have futons next to your desk to work from or an entire sleeping pod to yourself, to sleep in between shifts or "take a break". I have not worked at any of these, but I am sure you've seen a video or two on YouTube or one of those video platforms, of an engineer showing off a day in their life as an engineer for these tech giants. And if you haven't felt free to search one up, and you'll see what I am talking about. I remember graduating and that being the dream, working in a massive corporate campus, with all sorts of amenities you could think of, taking absolute advantage of these in every possible way. I think I even saw one of those Google engineers on YouTube take music lessons in the Google campus during her work break, which was insane to me. Anyway that was the dream prior to 2019, at least for myself I can say now that no amount of amenities is going to make me want to go back to working in an office setting anymore. Though we forcefully started working remotely in 2019 for about 2 years on average, I did not realize how much more of a convenience it was until I started doing it. There are also some cons to remote work, but I genuinely think the pros outweigh the cons by far. First I will start with the obvious pros of remote work, that being the commute time, gas spent going to and from the work office. Now this is a major benefit for those who are choosing to work at home, if you work remotely but spend lots of time traveling these days on the road then this pro may not be that big a deal to you anyway. In fact, it may not even be a pro as you may be potentially driving more depending on how often you travel via the road. Anyway this was the first immediate benefit I saw in remote work and I know some of my colleagues loved this as some had told me it would take them a solid hour to get to work everyday just because of traffic even though they lived only 30 minutes away. So they probably saved good on gas money and some road rage. The other benefit I personally experienced, and I feel this is more of a me thing, was the fact that I was able to concentrate significantly better at my home than in an office. I have already talked about this but again my home is dead silent, if there is an ant crawling on my floor

I will know about it, that is how quiet it is, and it really helps me when it comes to concentrating on a task. From experience, corporate offices tend to usually be loud, even if the cubicle you sit in is surrounded by walls they don't really do anything. You can always hear your next door neighbors when they are having a meeting at their desks or having a conversation with someone, and it has always been a pet peeve of mine because it is extremely distracting since these people sit less than a foot away from you. I am also guilty of this as there are not always rooms available to reserve for meetings, so I end up taking the meeting at my desk, and it is the most awkward thing ever. For this reason I feel I am much more productive and efficient in my home since there is no noise available to distract me, but that is just how I focus, I have met people in life who are the exact opposite and cannot live without noise. I also understand that being at home all the time can get irritating and make one feel some level of claustrophobia eventually, I know I reached this point myself. Even so, I still think remote work is a great and peaceful way to work, as you have the potential to travel where you please and work from the destination you have chosen. Just because you are working remotely it does not mean you have to work from the house all the time, unless explicitly told by your employer, but usually this restriction is at state level.

With this pandemic many remote roles as well as "digital nomad" programs have come to life, and I touched on this briefly, but the point is that if you want to travel and keep your career as a software engineer, then this is totally an option. These programs are not just for domestic travel but worldwide in select countries of course, you can also bring this up with your current employer to see what restrictions you may have when it comes to working from another location. Some companies like Spotify have truly embraced the remote workforce, that they've become extremely flexible when it comes to what city or state you want to work in. Some are still trying to get people back into the office, that have resorted to offering amenities and events that they did not offer prior to the pandemic. For example, my current employer wanted people to come to the office as of 2022 regardless of vaccination status, so they implemented amenities like free breakfast and lunch and now have happy hour events every Thursday after 4pm. In the end, very few people were still showing up, and the corporate policy came down to the employee having to be there in the office at least 3 days out of the week. However, from what I hear and see, people still show up when they please, or they need to, and to be honest, I can't blame them since many other companies have now emerged that are offering fully remote work. From my team alone, I know of at least 4 colleagues that left the company for an employer that was remote, even if that employer was not as big a name as the company they used to work for. In other words, I have witnessed people leave for remote roles, even if that means working for a startup or a completely volatile company. At any rate, this new "norm" of coming into the office 2 to 3 days a week are the corporations' attempts at getting people used to working in an office setting again. Be it to make their investors happy and therefore justify the lease these corporations have on the buildings they use as their corporate offices, or because of reasons I am just unaware of. Whatever the case, some of these corporations are being extremely pushy about their employees having to come to their offices, that are willing to look the other way when it comes to someone's vaccination status. Now I know this is a sensitive topic, so I promise not to touch much on it, but in some instances corporations are not making any exceptions for people who are not allowed to get vaccinated due to religion or other justifiable means. I personally know a coworker of mine that was ready to be let go, since he could not show up to the corporate office due to not being vaccinated because of his religion. The solution to this from a corporate standpoint was to mandate everyone be in the office regardless of whether or not they have taken a vaccine, but now this could potentially put those people in danger from my point of view. Anyway, these are the two most popular work models I have seen today which are working in a hybrid setting being 2 or 3 days a week in the office, or being a fully remote software engineer. I have yet to find a company that is software related, that is mandating their employees to show to their corporate office 5 days a week. I would not be surprised if I did find out that companies are already mandating their employers to come back to a full office week setting. As I have seen in the media, some CEOs, like Elon Musk for example, believe that remote workers just pretend to be working but appear less productive. I don't personally know if this is true as

I have no metric data to back this statement up, it could be true, or it could just be a justification for someone that likes to micromanage their employers, again I don't know. Don't get me wrong, I am all for in person work if that is what I am to experience once I show up to an in office setting. But if the only difference in collaboration when I show up is the usage of a physical whiteboard as opposed to the digital one from my laptop, then I see no value in me having to show up to the in person office setting. We are building software after all, not hardware, I also find it ridiculous to have to go to the office when the rest of my team members are scattered across the states or in my current situation, across the globe. The only person I see in the office is my manager, whom I rarely have to interact with and when I do, it is for a brief 15-minute call. The people I truly have to intensely collaborate with tend to be scattered throughout the globe and therefore the reason I just prefer to work remote, but that is just my 2 cents. Another great benefit I personally saw in remote work was the time being spent with loved ones without using up paid time off. I mean for holidays like Christmas or thanksgiving when I was fully remote I would drive a weekend to my hometown and work the work week from there, thus being able to save the vacation time, I would normally burn off on those holiday weeks. Since I was remote, I used it to my advantage and worked the weeks I would normally take off to travel to see family for the holidays. I guess you could say the pro was that I was working during these holiday weeks, but it was not much of a bother since I was also spending time with the family during and after the work shift, it was a win-win.

Anyhow, not everything is bunnies and flowers when it comes to remote work, there could be higher expectations from an employer since it is known that work is being done remotely. I know there were higher expectations on my end, at least at the start of the pandemic when everyone went to work fully remote. So let me explain, as I mentioned before my teammates are mostly scattered across the world, this means that I work with people in time zones where their day is my night and vice versa. Sometimes the work my teammates were assigned needed some sort of feedback or collaboration from me, but obviously this meant that they were either going to sacrifice their availability or I was. And in some cases I made myself available at 2 in the morning to help my teammates out, but this quickly got out of hand when I started getting messages at 12 am from that moment on. These people expected me to be randomly available whenever they needed me, irrespective of whether or not I completed my 8-hour shift for the day. It quickly became an expectation or trend, but I am thankful for this even as this is where I learned to be assertive with my time and health and set boundaries early on. Long story short, I took this to the manager, explained the situation and updated my calendar to show what hours of the day I was available. I also noted that if someone needs something from me, then it is them who need to adjust their schedule, not myself, and vice versa for when I need something. Anyway, problem solved, now I am only slacked or messaged during the hours I was hired to work for, but moral of the story is that people may assume you are available at any time of the day because you may be working in a remote setting. Another potential con of being a remote worker is micromanagement. What do I mean by that? I mean that the people you work with or under may want to digitally micromanage you, since they are not used to their employees being absent in their presence. This almost happened to me, but it happened to a coworker of mine before the case made its way onto human resources and then our manager, so it never ended up happening to me. What had happened was that a coworker of mine who was an associate engineer at the time was collaborating on a project with a more senior engineer, who was not used to ever working in a remote setting. This senior engineer wanted to monitor the associate's work from that moment on every step of the way, the associate was asked to share his screen for the entire 8 hour shift monitoring every little thing done during each shift. This of course did not sit well with the associate and took it to the higher ups, to get the problem addressed. Remote work can be daunting for those whose entire 20 year experience in the industry has always been in person, but the world of technology is one that evolves very frequently, and I think the workforce needs to evolve with it to stay relevant. I mean really, there is like a new iPhone released every year and a new version of a programming language every six months or sometimes even less, it is ridiculous. But these are some of the cons I have heard about or experienced on my own being, availability assumption and micromanagement problems from employers. I'm sure there may be others, just like there are many other pros to remote work that I did not mention. I will say this though, and this may be a negative for some folks, but no amount of amenities or work events, seem like a good motivation for me to want to go back and work in an in office setting. There may be people out there who think otherwise and really appreciate the free lunches their employers give them, not that I don't. It is just that for me nothing beats remorse work because not only can I spend time with loved ones while I work but work also as I travel, saving my vacation days for bigger splurge adventures.

Remote Work Is Here to Stay

Is remote here to stay? Absolutely freaking yes! I definitely think so, I truly believe that the companies who are currently following a hybrid or fully in office model will eventually offer remote positions. I think this probably will make the most financial sense for those corporations that lease or have invested in corporate offices for their employees to use. As those corporate buildings will be expensive to keep, and may after all turn out somewhat redundant, if the role at hand has been proven to be reasonably doable remotely In such a case, I don't just see a transition to the remote workforce a win for the employee, it is probably just a big a win or bigger for the employer. And from a financial standpoint there may be companies that will still offer an equipment budget to their employees, which may add up, but keep in mind that these corporations set the budget, so it may still be a cheaper option and renewing an office building lease. After all, real estate prices have risen to a quite notable difference since 2019, and we have yet to see a steady decline to "pre-pandemic" prices. Do note though, as I have said many times here that I am not an entrepreneur in any sense, so my gut feeling could totally be off here. Regardless, those employers that are offering remote roles will probably be stealing a lot of talent for other corporations to still remain working in the office. Just a hunch though, corporate is very powerful especially in capitalist America, so you never know. I read somewhere "on the internet" that when Elon Musk took over twitter, he began working out plans to get rid of the free lunch offered at Twitter. His reason being was that twitter was that the estimated cost per lunch served at Twitter was totaling somewhat over 400 dollars, which from his perspective did not make sense as most people were working remotely. So, this will definitely be something corporations will probably take into consideration if they decide to transition to a remote available option. Also, the only reason I brought this up is to make the people working at the fancy offices with many "free" perks aware of something that can potentially be taken away or no longer be free if their employee decides to offer remote work environments. Not sure how this may affect "team building" events, but I would not be surprised if corporations decide to also cut back on these "team building" activities, when moving into a remote work environment.

One last thing, I would take into account when it comes to remote work, are the restrictions that may come with such a role. For example, I have spoken to companies that are offering "remote" roles as new openings come to life in their organization. And although these types of roles look exciting on paper as one might be thinking, great, I can now work from wherever I please. Not so fast, it turns out some of these roles have state restrictions, I found this to be especially common with startup like companies. What I mean to say is that even though these roles are marketed as remote roles, which technically they are, the employee may be restricted to working only from the states which the employer allows. So if you were hoping to hop around different cities throughout the US or even abroad to work remotely, you may be limited to how far you can travel to change your work setting. I don't have any further specifics as to whether or not one could get away with this by using a virtual private network, in order to simulate that one is working from an employer's approved location, but that is something to think about or ask if the opportunity arises. The only other thing I can say is that, when human resources from the company I spoke to tried to tell me why these restrictions were in place, it sounded like the reasons behind this were somewhat IRS related. As I always say it never hurts to try, so if you end up in the remote role of your dreams, but your hope was to travel and get to know your country and the world while you work then it may be a good idea to ask your employer about any travel restrictions set in stone and ways around them if they exist. When I build software I like to ask for forgiveness instead of permission, but when it comes to an employer if I had landed my dream role, I'd probably exercise caution above all else when it comes to travel and work.

Work Trends and Controversies

As one can imagine with the lovely internet at the disposal of mankind, amidst the ongoing pandemic battle that started in 2019, came the inevitable memes and trends about remote work. One such major trend that took off was what is referred to as "quiet quitting". This term is used to describe an employee or white collar worker that does only what is necessary and nothing more, to fulfill their duties at their role. Meaning that the employee is completely unsubscribed from "hustle" culture, which translates to no longer looking at work as a form of lifestyle. If this sounds confusing, don't worry, it really isn't. All this "quiet quitting" thing is trying to say or the message that it is trying to convey is that the employee does not and is not under any circumstance interested in going above and beyond when it comes to their work performance. This does not mean such employees are absent from fulfilling their job, it just means that they will only do what is needed to fulfill their duties at their role. This is my interpretation of such a trend, and I can say that this quickly became popular due to the raise for concern in "mental health". And if you ask me, the raise for concepts around poor mental health probably came from the lockdowns and remote roles introduced during the pandemic. There were many factors at hand, but perhaps one of the more obvious ones was a disadvantage of working remotely. Being the expectation of being available for work during any time of the day, any day, when one is working from the comfort of their home as many were in 2020 and 2021. And this, of course, was anticipated as industries that have never before even thought of attempting to offer remote work, made the drastic transitions to keep their business moving during a crisis. It was do or die when the pandemic hit, and unfortunately in this chaos some companies were just not big enough to thrive through the virus and its lockdown protocols. Others, however, decided to swim in whatever means necessary, even if it meant working in a remote setting that had never been done before in their own organization. This of course lead to poor remote work experience for first timers through the use of micromanagement, sharing live screens for entire shifts, messaging people at 8 or 10 pm or as desired for work related subjects etcetera. As a result of at least 2 forceful years of people not getting out of the house and also working from it, only stepping out for essential activities, mental health became an additional concern aside from the physical. I will admit, though, that most of the people I see, who chose to raise a voice over these types of concerns, are the millennials and generation z. Though from my experience there are concerns around mental health with the older generations, it is more common with the upcoming generations and I see they tend to be much more vocal about things for mental health and such. I myself do not consider myself an activist, though I am of the millennial generation, but acting as such has become more and more of a trend among the younger generations from my perspective. Don't get me wrong, I am all for "quiet quitting" in every sense of the word, especially when the individual needs a job to survive on and what they are working on does not excite them, or maybe it does but is not their dream to move up the corporate ladder. But I must admit I thought this was something that was already done, subconsciously at the quiet level, meaning you would work as such but not preach about it to the world, but I guess times have changed. To be quite honest I see no added benefit to preaching such a concept to the world, as I mentioned before this seems to me like something that was already done, in an actual hush type of manner. So I think if anything this may make it more difficult for newcomers to get hired, if they come into the industry preaching to a potential employer about "quiet quitting" when they're interviewed. I'm all for offering career advice and making the new generations aware of things that may be in their best interest, after all that is what I am trying to accomplish in this book, but not sure if preaching about such concepts is a smart move from that perspective. Anyway just my 2 cents as always, I will note that as I stated sometime back in one of the prior sections, there may be instances where it may actually be in one's interest to actually go above and beyond in one's role if that is a way of moving up within an organization. I understand that this type of scenario can be rare, and therefore one of many reasons why I myself am pro "quiet quitting". As I have said before, once you've entered the world of being employed as a corporate employee, the game turns into one of longevity, meaning as long as one continues to do their job as expected, the raise or promotion will come with due time. And I literally mean due time, as most companies require their employees and candidates to accumulate x amount of years of work experience to move up the ladder or become eligible for a salary increase of any kind. Assuming the employee's performance is to the standards specified of course, which is somewhat difficult to screw up as I have explained, all one has to do is their job and nothing more. Anyway, don't mean to sound like a broken record, I just wanted to make the connection to this "quiet quitting" concept based on my observation and experiences.

Sometime immediately after the pandemic occurred, an economic trend known as "the great resignation" was another big concept that caught my eye. Unlike the cultural trend we just discussed, this one actually acts on its words. The great resignation refers to employees voluntarily leaving their employment during the pandemic, because of the effects of the pandemic. I don't have data to back this up so what I am about to say is based on the very little research I have done in the past and the brief amount of news sessions I have watched. Anyhow, the reasons behind employees willingly leaving such corporations during the pandemic were because of things like inflexibility of remote work opportunities, wage adjustments to account for inflation, raising cost of living etcetera. All the reasons which seem to be tied directly or indirectly with the pandemic as the source of these events. So as you can see, though a very contagious virus forced many governments and organizations to either shut down or work in a remote setting, not all corporations were willing to make the transition. Understandably, this raised many health concerns for employees who were still required to show up and work among many of their co-workers in an enclosed building. Additionally, as one can imagine since many people began working remotely, home prices began to rise up over the course of those two years. Though inflation kicked in, salary wage adjustments are usually not required to be made to counter inflation, so if you find yourself to be employed by a company that does actually do this, consider yourself extremely lucky. So this meant that the cost of living rose for many folks, but the pay granted by employees did not change, so people naturally decided to look elsewhere for pay that met their needs. As I said before, some corporations remained extremely stubborn for one reason or another and refused to change their business model to a remote work environment, to adjust to the ongoing events of the world. Some of these businesses did not live long and some inevitably had to eventually adapt, and yes there were other monster corporations who were still thriving during this pandemic and great resignation event. But these are just a few of many reasons employees chose to move to different employers, whose compensation and company values better aligned with the employees' new goals and interest at hand. Obviously this was not something that came out of the blue but rather a type of domino effect because of what the pandemic initiated for many corporations and the workforce industry.

SO, SHOULD YOU BECOME A SOFTWARE ENGINEER?

By now, we have touched on the routes one can take as a software engineer, and have gotten a glimpse as to some of the roles I have worked in the industry. Roles like mobile, web development, software consulting, and life as a software tester. Hopefully this gave a general overview of what working in some of these roles has to offer for someone. For me personally, the roles in my career that I have enjoyed the most so far, not counting remote roles (because that was temporary for me) are the role of software consulting and the role as a mobile engineer. I will start first with what I liked most in these roles, and then make my transition over to what I really didn't look forward to in my day to day in each role. The goal of describing my favorite roles so far as an engineer and the experiences they brought me, is to provide further insight as to whether or not this career is a good path to pursue for someone or not. Everyone's goals and interests are different, and therefore hopefully these experiences can serve as a tool to more or less see what one can expect when working as a software engineer for a living. Though I actually enjoy the act of constructing software for a living, a lot of the reasons why I ended up liking this career path not only had to do with passion, but also with things in life that I enjoy doing other than building software. After all, most people and hopefully everyone in this world has a life outside of work. So my advice to you, the reader, of the upcoming sections, is to ask yourself as you read, what your long term goals are and what things you enjoy doing in life and analyze if the experiences I describe align with your interests and needs or not. I think this will help form some kind of basis as to whether or not this type of career is worth considering giving a shot for an individual or not.

What I Personally Like & Dislike

Ok so for starters consulting had first caught my attention for reasons that were very exciting to me, which involved travel, and the opportunity to work on very distinct projects. For as long as I can remember, even prior to the pandemic, travel has always been something I have always taken an interest in. Not sure if this is because I have always been a "city rat" or because I rarely traveled out of my hometown prior to starting my software career, but every time I got to discover a new city, I became suspended in awe. So when I started working as a consultant, prior to the pandemic arriving, as I mentioned before I was shipped back and forth to and from a different city depending on the project I got allocated. To many people who are looking to purchase a home and settle in one city for the rest of their lives and start a family, this may not be the most appealing lifestyle, as it may not align with the goals set for these individuals. I however felt super fortunate at the time, to have had a job as an engineering consultant that enabled me to stay in a different city for the duration of the project lifespan to which I was allocated to. Keep in mind that I also grew up in what felt like a very small to midsize city, with hardly any green color surrounding me. So when I got shipped to larger metroplex cities with staggeringly tall buildings and forest-like nature surrounding them, I could not help but fill myself with joy by the sight alone. Additionally, when it came to projects I wanted to work in, not only did I get to choose what type of projects to take on based on my interest, but was also given the opportunity to choose based on location that I wished to visit. I may or may have already gotten over how consulting companies map their employees to software projects for their clients, but I will note that not all consulting firms operate like this. Some firms rather operate by mapping their employees to client projects based on need or based on the employee's strengths and skills. The firm I worked for operated like this, but also allowed for flexibility in negotiating the projects that the individual was interested in, which made me feel really fortunate. Though, in the end, there were few projects of interest for me to choose from. Having that option to swap around different projects with different types of technologies is something that may not be very common in the corporate workplaces. If, for example, you wanted the opportunity to work in website development with the React technology or say perhaps in something related to the python programming language, then your manager would try and get you placed in projects related to such technologies. If I make it seem so great, then why did I end up leaving, right? Why leave when you are somewhere you are happy. Well the answer to this is very simple, though my income was finally stable at the time, I was not satisfied with the pay and benefits I had, I wanted to move up the ladder, I wanted to reach my goal of making double what I was getting paid at the time. As I said before, not everything is bunnies and flowers in this life and though working for a consulting firm brought me joy at the time, there were things I was not happy with. Besides pay, the other bothersome factor I came across when working in consulting was the company dynamic around travel expenses. When people were shipped to new cities, that usually meant they left a house or apartment they lived in behind to go pay for rent or a hotel in the new city they were shipped to. This meant that during the duration of the project one was working on at the client's location, the consultant was having to pay rent in this location as well as the mortgage or rent they left behind in their home city. Furthermore, these consultants were only reimbursed when they came back from the client's location, which really depended on the duration of the project they were working on. So this meant that at any point in time that one was employed with this particular consulting firm, the employee had to have extra cushion money on the side for when they got shipped to work from a client's location. As much as I liked travel, this quickly became a major disadvantage, and called for a team up with other work colleagues that got mapped to the same project, to be able to share a house together at the client's location in an effort to decrease our travel expenses. Now that I look back at it, this may have been one of the root causes of me wanting to move up the corporate ladder in an effort to better afford the travel expenses I was forced to take. I will note though that sharing a house with a bunch of coworkers for travel was very fun at the time and felt as if I was living in some sort of college frat house. Some of those coworkers actually became lifelong friends. I will also say that my job as a consultant caused me a lot of anxiety from time to time, specifically around the process of being mapped to a project. The project allocation process was as follows, when a project comes up that both the client and consultant have a mutual interest in working on, the client undergoes a series of interview questions made by the client. The purpose of these questions is not only to assess if the consultant's skills will be needed in the project of interest, but also to determine whether or not the consultant is capable of handling such a project. Sounds fair enough, right? So why the anxiety? Well, here is the deal, the way these interviews were conducted was by literally following the same interview process that these corporations use for hiring full time employers at their company directly. I mean to say that more often than not the interviews were broken down into stages as described in the "interview preparation" section of this book. There were entire 8-hour days of interviews scheduled for consultants, where the client's assessed their technical, soft and behavioral skills in order to approve said consultant to the project of interest. I later looked at this as an advantage to advance my career and use those interview experiences as practice for making the transition from consultant to full time work with one particular company, and it ended up working after an unimaginable amount of trial and error.

One final thing I will address is company internal organization, this is one of those things I rarely see a company be good at. With the exception of 1 corporation I have worked with, literally every other employer I have had has had their fair share of organization challenges. In their defense, though, I think this type of thing is expected when companies as gigantic as Verizon or Sony have teams within their organization that they never even heard of. I mean, they become so large at scale to the point where literally every feature in their system has an entire team behind it. However, I will admit that some companies are extremely noticeably more disorganized than others, and that can cause the employee to have a discouraging or poor work experience. When I mean organization I mean just that, things like ad-hoc meetings just about every day, status update meetings that turn into war rooms or troubleshooting sessions randomly. Missing deadlines not because the employees are lazy or ignorant, but simply because there is a lack of proper collaboration and communication from all levels of the workplace, from leadership all the way down to developers themselves. These are some of the disadvantages I have seen take place when new teams are being formed as there is lack of direction from either leadership, the company or both. So this was just a couple of notes of other things that were not as enjoyable in my career and these are likely scenarios an individual is likely to experience especially when first starting out in any career. Though these experiences were not pleasant, I am grateful to them as they have made me grow in the industry and as a human being, helping me develop a sense of character within myself.

So what about mobile development? I did mention mobile development was among one of my most pleasant roles I have had throughout my career, so here is a quick gist on what I liked and disliked about it. Most about what I liked in this role was tied to the type of technology I was using, let me begin by saying that I have always been a big fan of apple products. Not all of them, but I would say that I like about 80 percent of the products Apple has to offer, So when I landed the role of mobile IOS development at the university I graduated from back then, I became filled with excitement to be able to build apps made specifically for iPhone devices. I was not only happy about having to learn Apple's native programming language and development environment system, but was also intrigued at the fact that customers would be able to pull whatever application I built on the phone that rested in the palm of their hands. I quickly became filled with passion and joy every day that I would walk into work in order to complete the application my superiors had assigned to me to. The technology was amazing to me because it had me learning how to manipulate and construct the arms and legs of the software that operated the phone, aka the applications of an iPhone device. Not only that but I was working on applications that were requested by the university's human resource department which made me even happier knowing that there would already be an audience willing to use the app requested at hand. This was a very rewarding experience as this work experience paved the way to kick start my career as a full time software professional. I say this because though this role was a part-time internship role, it gave me a great glimpse as to what to expect when transitioning into full time work in the software area. It showed me what it was like to not only work with technologies I was passionate about, but how to work in a team of engineers to bring to life a product requested by clientele. It also taught me how to gather and interpret requirements, as well as how the corporate processes work and how team collaboration helps meet deadlines set for launching software products to a live environment. That said, I don't think I have any negative things to say about my time as an IOS mobile development engineer, due to the fact that this was my very first internship and exposure to a real life setting of the software work industry. The only cons I could think of are that this role was an internship which usually means either no pay, or very low pay compared to what full time personnel gets, but this is not specific to software. At any rate, it was a humble and extremely fortunate experience to have during my route to becoming a full time software engineer.

If I Had to Start Over

If I had to start over, would I? In all honesty, probably not, or at least that is what I tell myself most days. I will admit that the pandemic has made me question many life choices when it comes to my career, but it seems like this is something that has affected most people I have talked to, and more on that later. Anyway, after a deep dive evaluation, I'd probably still have taken the same route I took to end up working as a software engineer for a living.

My number one reason for this, is the fact that I am finally paid for doing something that I enjoy, at least remotely enough to where I can see myself doing this for a very long time, and possibly my entire life. And don't get me wrong, I mean sure this is the most rewarding career I've ever had in terms of compensation, benefits package, flexibility etcetera. They are great, but I will say that the older I get, the more I realize that what matters most is finding a way to be truly happy on a day-to-day basis. Therefore, if technology is not something that peaks one's interest, especially when it comes to working among teams, then I strongly discourage it, as this can potentially be something one end up working on for the rest of their lives. If this is not the case, though, then I encourage pursuing the field, but always try and ask yourself the following questions as an upcoming engineer. Is this something I would like to work on? Assuming I would work from home, would this be something exciting enough for me to want to make the effort of getting out of bed and logging into my laptop? Or would I simply log in to my work laptop from my bed under the covers, half asleep? Do I want to work from home? Maybe an in office setting is better suited for me or a digital nomad type of gig? Do I have enough energy to deal with people I don't enjoy speaking with today? Do I have to talk to people today? Can I just code my life away until my shift ends? That would be great. I know some of these can seem kind of corny, but you may be surprised at how often these questions are made from my and my colleagues' perspective everyday we wake up to work. I guess the message that I am trying to convey here is, move forward with pursuing software or any other career, but only if you truly enjoy doing it. You don't have to be extremely passionate about it or obsessed, but I would suggest at least liking what you do, even if it is just a little bit. Otherwise, the career may feel like a long miserable drag of a job that is just there to help pay the bills, and that does not at all feel like freedom or joy. I have been there, and I can confirm, even if you are compensated fairly it does not balance out or at least it did not for me. In my experience, it is better to have to work in something you are interested in and be compensated fairly, than to be compensated unfairly working at a place you can't stand being in. This may just be common sense, but my prior gigs serve me as a gentle reminder of how fortunate I have become to end up working in the line of software, and therefore when I ask myself if I'd start over in an entirely different field my answer ends up being no. I will set some things straight though, notice how I use the word like and do my best to avoid saying things like "follow your passion", this "needs to be your passion". I do this for a very specific reason and that is that, like me, there are many people out there who are as old as I am or much older and still don't know what their true passion is. And that is totally fine, it is a blessing for someone to discover their passion early on in life, but not everyone is as lucky. As I said many times I like tech I can even go as far as to say that I actually love it, but passion for me goes beyond that level, and I'd be lying if I'd say I love every minute of working as a software engineer for a corporation that is more than happy to replace me the day it becomes their best interest to do so. My true love for work in the industry comes from time actually dealing with the technical side of things, and not necessarily the people or corporate pro-cess set in place that one has to follow. I'm talking about the days or partial hours of my daily work life where I spend my day coding and problem-solving as opposed to attending numerous meetings and or "leadership" update conferences. That is the portion of my workday that I look forward to every day, and for whatever reason I was not born a people guy, I tend to find people draining. This is probably the reason I am not fond of meetings, especially when the problem at hand can be solved via email or with a one line text message, this tends to be much faster too. Anyway, not all meetings are bad, some can be useful, but I notice that these useful meetings take place when "pair programming sessions" take place within a team, as I find the participants of the pair programming session to often exchange very useful technical knowledge and learn wonders from one another. See it is the exchange of knowledge in problem-solving, or technical skills that I look forward to in those types of meetings. For those that don't know pair programming is exactly what it sounds like, this usually means two people at a single desktop or laptop, working together "programming" to solve a software issue, both getting and giving feedback to how the problem at hand is to be solved. So my love for tech is one of the biggest reasons I would not switch careers if I had to start over, as it is among one of my few interests with the logical potential to help me make a decent living.

Second but also just as important I would say is the flexibility that came with this career. I am referring to work-life balance, it has been the best I have ever had, when it comes to my years of experience as a software professional. Now this is something that can vary from company to company, but out of the 4 I have worked with so far, not a single one of them has given me serious trouble when it comes to work-life balance. There are exceptions to this but in the end I have noticed everything more than balances out, and I will clarify. When I say there are exceptions I don't mean that there are instances where work actually does get in the way of life, well I do, but not in the manner that one might think of. For example, if something breaks in production on a Friday night or say Sunday morning, and you are the engineer that is called to solve the problem since you or your team were responsible for said product. Then yeah, you may be stuck fixing things up on a Sunday night until you are done. So the moral of the story is to always write quality code! Not just kidding of course but if such a thing were to happen not to worry, the employer usually lets you subtract those hours worked from your normal work week or as applicable, especially since overtime is rarely encouraged from my experience. If an employer or manager is actually forcing overtime without actually letting you take time off for extra hours worked previously then that is not only a red flag, but an example of what work-life balance disruption is. Anyhow, as I said before things tend to really balance out in the long run, I have had weeks where my workload would translate to 50 hours plus or more work weeks, but then the following two months turn out to be 20 hour work weeks. So it just depends on the stage of the projects being worked on, their maturity and need for enhancement among many other variables. I can't promise that every software company out there works in a similar manner to this, but this has been my personal experience, after being with four different employers. Part of the flexibility this career offers also has to do with autonomy, again from my experience, and I don't know if I have just been fortunate enough to have had good managers or what, but autonomy is heavily encouraged. I mean autonomy in every sense of the word. I am referring to things as simple as to what time one goes into work physically or otherwise to things as deep and complex as in what direction to take a software project assigned at hand for the company's best interest. This however, can sometimes be a double-edged sword as oftentimes I need clear direction from management or leadership, as to what direction to stir the project assigned at hand. And if I go the route I am not supposed to or solve the problem at hand in a manner that is not most beneficial for long term company goals, which I am usually unaware of, this can end up meaning rework for me or loss of trust in my abilities to perform. On the other hand if I get it right then it could mean new doors have opened to more career growth opportunities but regardless of the outcome this is also a great work learning experience, which is why I framed autonomy a double-edged sword.

The last reason for sticking to software still after being given the opportunity to start over is the compensation. I do my best to play a humble human being, and I am, but the fact of the matter is that the world we live in runs on money, so compensation will always be a deciding factor until then. Throughout my entire life my career as a software engineer has not only been the most rewarding in terms of career growth but also in terms of compensation and vacation time. That said, if it wasn't for the compensation this career has brought to me, I would not have been able to do many of the things I like to do in life whether it be for me, my family or loved ones, so there is a lot to be thankful for there. I don't mean to sound like an advertiser but if you are looking for a well paid career that involves coding or anything software related, without having to go through the hassle of attaining a master's or a PhD degree, to be compensated fairly, then look no further, and consider a career as a software engineer.

CONCLUSION

Great, you've made it this far! So now that you have an insight as to what a day in the life as a software engineer looks like, you are free to make your own analysis as to whether or not pursuing a software career makes sense for you. These motives can be driven by passion, flexibility or simply money, or perhaps something other than the reasons listed. If you are still undecided however, don't sweat it, you can always come back and give it a try at a later stage in life. I know many people I work with who did not start working in software until they reached a much later stage in their lives. Anyhow, hopefully this book provided at least some sense of useful insight into career paths, remote work opportunities, pros and cons of working in software and ways to break into a software engineering role. Do keep in mind though, that this book offered an extremely narrow and brief overview of what the industry can look like, as this was based on my five years of experience of working as an engineer. Also note that the industry is forever evolving and things may look very different six months down the road from the writing of this book in 2022. That could be for the better or for the worse, there may be more branches of software one can branch out to or maybe less, as artificial intelligence seems to be coming up on the rise. By the time this is read the amount of remote roles may have doubled or tripled, only time will tell. Anyway, with that I conclude the topics of this book in hopes that these experiences can serve as reference to determine what career path is best pursued for someone. Thank you again for making it this far out, and the best of wishes in future endeavors, and career paths pursued.